HOW TO STUDY LITERATURE
General Editors: John Peck and Martin Coyle

HOW TO STUDY A D. H. LAWRENCE NOVEL

IN THE SAME SERIES

How to Study a Novel *John Peck*
Literary Terms and Criticism *John Peck and Martin Coyle*
How to Study a Shakespeare Play *John Peck and Martin Coyle*
How to Begin Studying English Literature *Nicholas Marsh*
How to Study a Jane Austen Novel *Vivien Jones*
How to Study a Thomas Hardy Novel *John Peck*
How to Study a Renaissance Play *Chris Coles*
How to Study Modern Drama *Kenneth Pickering*
How to Study a Poet *John Peck*
How to Study Chaucer *Rob Pope*
How to Study Romantic Poetry *Paul O'Flinn*
How to Study a Charles Dickens Novel *Keith Selby*

IN PREPARATION

How to Study Contemporary Poetry *Tony Curtis*
How to Study a Joseph Conrad Novel *Brian Spittles*
How to Study an E. M. Forster Novel *Nigel Messenger*

HOW TO STUDY A D. H. LAWRENCE NOVEL

Nigel Messenger

MACMILLAN

First published 1989

Published by
MACMILLAN EDUCATION LTD
Houndmills, Basingstoke, Hampshire RG21 2XS
and London
Companies and representatives
throughout the world

Printed in Hong Kong

British Library Cataloguing in Publication Data
Messenger, Nigel
How to study a D. H. Lawrence novel. —
(How to study literature).
1. Fiction in English. Lawrence, D. H.
(David Herbert). 1885–1930. Study
techniques
I. Title II. Series
823′.912
ISBN 0–333–42862–5

Contents

General editors' preface

EVERYBODY who studies literature, either for an examination or simply for pleasure, experiences the same problem: how to understand and respond to the text. As every student of literature knows, it is perfectly possible to read a book over and over again and yet still feel baffled and at a loss as to what to say about it. One answer to this problem, of course, is to accept someone else's view of the text, but how much more rewarding it would be if you could work out your own critical response to any book you choose or are required to study.

The aim of this series is to help you develop your critical skills by offering practical advice about how to read, understand and analyse literature. Each volume provides you with a clear method of study so that you can see how to set about tackling texts on your own. While the authors of each volume approach the problem in a different way, every book in the series attempts to provide you with some broad ideas about the kind of text you are likely to be studying and some broad ideas about how to think about literature; each volume then shows you how to apply these ideas in a way which should help you construct your own analysis and interpretation. Unlike most critical books, therefore, the books in this series do not simply convey someone else's thinking about a text, but encourage you and show you how to think about a text for yourself.

Each book is written with an awareness that you are likely to be preparing for an examination, and therefore practical advice is given not only on how to understand and analyse literature, but also on how to organise a written response. Our hope is that, although these books are intended to serve a practical purpose, they may also enrich your enjoyment of literature by making you a more confident reader, alert to the interest and pleasure to be derived from literary texts.

John Peck
Martin Coyle

Acknowledgements

I SHOULD like to thank my colleagues in the Humanities Department at Oxford Polytechnic for their encouragement, especially Paul O'Flinn and Rob Pope, who gave me good advice, and Colin Pedley, who checked the typescript. My special thanks are due to Tina Duffelen-Weller, who deciphered my handwriting and did the typing. I should like to acknowledge the generous support and constructive criticism of the general editors of this series.

To Jenny, Marcus, Timothy
and Abigail

1

Approaching a Lawrence novel

Let us imagine that you have just read a novel by D. H. Lawrence. The chances are that you will have enjoyed it, for Lawrence is one of the great authors of English literature who is also popular and whose novels are very widely read. Things will have puzzled you, but the experience should have been more pleasurable than painful. Yet your enjoyment might be somewhat difficult to reconcile with the fact that you are going to have to study this same novel for an exam. Similarly, while you might feel that the problems Lawrence addresses are directly relevant to your own life, you may also be aware that he has the reputation of being a difficult and obscure author. Moreover, he seems to excite strong feelings of a positive or negative nature. Obviously it is not going to be easy sorting out what you are 'supposed to think' in order to do well in the exam.

That's the nub of the problem, isn't it? How can you read honestly and write truthfully about the book given the strains of an exam? The temptation is simply to give your examiners what you think they want rather than what you actually feel. The fact of the matter, however, is that you will never write well and give of your best – and so do well in the exam – unless you write honestly, and unless you find your own response and build your own reading of the text. The aim of this book is to help you do just this. Reading and studying a complex text is, of course, hard work, but it can also be stimulating and enjoyable. It needs to be done in a systematic way, but there is room for intuition and discovery. Above all, literary criticism is an active, investigative process. It should not be just a matter of passive absorption and reproduction of received ideas. 'Truth' is not given but made: a good essay is an act of persuasion to the writer's point of view.

As you approach a Lawrence novel it might help to remember that the text you are studying was produced by another human being with problems of his own. Lawrence was a miner's son emancipated out of his class by his education. He was the first major English novelist with a working-class background and lived through the turbulent years of political unrest, social change and war in the first quarter of this century. It would be extraordinary if these stresses and strains did not find expression in his novels. The 'classic' text you are going to read, or have just read, no doubt comes complete with scholarly introduction, notes and bibliography, but it was certainly not the effortless inspiration of genius. All Lawrence's major novels are the result of much revision and redrafting; if they are sometimes difficult to read, it is worth understanding that they were not easy to write either. They may be full of unresolved difficulties that cannot be ignored or smoothed away.

I have said that Lawrence excites very strong responses in readers. If you go too soon to the great variety of critical material available, you will be amazed, and confused, by the versions of Lawrence that exist. To some of his immediate contemporaries he was, quite literally, a madman or degenerate, and his books were banned. In the middle years of this century he was praised as a highly moral writer, unrivalled in his ability to explore man's relationship with nature, his fellow beings, and his own inner life. More recently he has been regarded as a sexist writer by feminists; they see clearly defined patterns of male dominance and female submission in his texts and find these offensive. All the more reason, then, that you get your own basic ideas sorted out before you go looking for collaborative evidence or challenging alternatives.

If you have just finished your first Lawrence novel, you are bound to have had some problems. It might reassure you if I make a list of some of the major difficulties I have experienced. They may be similar to yours.

The lack of an obvious plot

We expect novels to tell stories that are either ordinary or extraordinary. In other words, we look to a novel to entertain us with an exciting narrative involving intrigue, suspense, adventure and romance, often in remote locations, or to give us a more sombre exploration of ordinary life and ordinary problems. There is a sense in which Lawrence does not quite fit into either category. Lawrence is interested in ordinary experiences but treats them in an exotic and highly dramatic way. It could be said that everything and nothing 'happens' in a Lawrence novel, because he is preoccupied with the common experiences we all share: childhood, adolescence, courtship, love relationships and marriage, family life and death. This new subject matter, hitherto marginalised or ignored by novelists, does not seem to lend itself to the usual kind of plot development. If your initial reading experience of a Lawrence novel was anything like mine, you will have found it difficult to see how the text hangs together or spot any clear pattern of development in the story. One responds to a series of vividly rendered episodes that do not seem very obviously related to each other. Indeed, there is a sense of repetition, of 'going round in circles', that can get confusing, even rather tedious and boring.

A new conception of character

Lawrence's characters are not solid, stable and consistent. They are difficult to describe externally, fix to a social role or sum up in a few words. They often seem confused or uncertain why they are doing things. Contradiction is built into them and they seem unable to act coherently within a range of clearly perceived options. As readers, we are drawn into them; we experience as they experience and this can be very enthralling, but then it is difficult to stand outside and judge them. We cannot fit them into some sort of moral scheme or tell whether they are supposed to be 'good' or 'bad'. We do not seem to be given any reliable criteria for assessing them, and this is very disorienting.

Difficulties of language and style

Lawrence's language can seem loose and vague but, at other times, dense and highly textured. It moves between extremes. When he is writing about nature, natural processes and the material world generally, he is capable of extraordinary lyricism and has a sharp eye for detail. But when he writes about his characters' inner state of mind – their feelings and ideas – he can be very obscure and difficult. I think you will find that one of the main characteristics of Lawrence's language is this movement between the highly concrete and particularised, and the philosophically abstract. The texts are marked by sudden disconcerting shifts between the external world of society and nature, and the internal world of the characters' psychology.

Lawrence writes 'poetically': by this I mean that he often uses language in a very inventive way, stretching words outside their normal contexts and usages in an attempt to express new modes of thought and feeling. This makes for demanding reading. He prefers, like a poet, to express himself metaphorically and symbolically rather than logically and directly. This is not reassuring for us, his readers, because we feel called upon to construct our own meanings without much direct authorial guidance. Sometimes we feel worked on by Lawrence without understanding quite how or why. We do not feel in control and this is unsettling. We are pulled into experiences as they occur; we are made to live through them with the characters at moments of great tension, emotional turmoil and heightened dramatic excitement where Lawrence's syntax mines the ebb and flow, the uncertainty and provisionality, of life itself. Readers expecting a more conventional kind of fiction can react in a rather hostile way to this and their criticism is often directed at Lawrence's style. he is accused of being 'vague', 'repetitious' and 'rhetorical'. He is often all of these things without, necessarily, being a bad writer.

I have tried to summarise some of my initial difficulties under these broad headings and I hope they accord with some of your own. If you have found your Lawrence novel exciting in places but also rather confusing in others and the book as a whole seemed a shapeless mess, you are only responding honestly: many other readers have felt this same mixture of admiration and irritation. But how can we begin to make some sense of it all? Is there some framework or overview that can help us place Lawrence as a novelist, compare him with other novelists, and enable us to work out what is distinctive about his contribution to the novel as a form? I think there is. In any novel there is always a tension between individual characters and the society in which they have to live.

The tension between the individual and society

All novelists are preoccupied with the relationship between the individual characters and the society in which they have to live and shape their existence and seek some measure of fulfilment. A common pattern used by novelists concerned with social injustice, for example, is the story of a poor or disinherited person who struggles to overcome the obstacles that society puts in his (or her) path. He learns to make the best of his chances, to distinguish between true and false friends, and finally win through to fame and fortune. A more subtle variation of this pattern used by novelists more interested in psychology and the interior life is the story of a rather wilful, unself-knowing person who makes unreasonable demands on life, is disciplined by society and through suffering learns some measure of wisdom and acceptance. A tragic version of this plot pattern often makes the reader sympathetic to the demands of the hero or heroine, who nevertheless is left alone outside society or even dead at the end of the story.

Does this tension and its accompanying plot patterns exist in the Lawrence novel you have just read?

I think you will find that it does, though in a rather unusual way. Whatever the Lawrence novel you've read, isn't it true that the main characters never really find a reassuring place in society at the end of the book? Isn't it the case that the tension between the individual and society remains unresolved and a source of potentially tragic conflict? Society in Lawrence is finally seen as hostile and unwelcoming, but it is also true that Lawrence makes us aware of untamed, wild areas in the human personality that the individual can never master or fully express in a social role. Hence the importance of nature for Lawrence. I am sure you have noticed that he writes about nature in a particularly charged and significant manner. The individual in nature is as important for Lawrence as the individual in society. By showing men and women relating intimately to nature, natural processes and natural rhythms, Lawrence is highlighting those aspects of human personality and human need that can never be fully expressed through our social identity. Our natural selves are seen to be in constant struggle against our social selves. The tension between self and society is being reworked by Lawrence in new and challenging ways.

If Lawrence believes in this inevitable conflict it is not difficult to understand why we feel morally lost sometimes: there is no code based on our modern social organisation that could accommodate such a belief. There are powerful, untamed forces in Lawrence's fiction that are a source of great creativity, but also of great destruction and inevitable unhappiness. They are the source of Lawrence's disturbing power that we can sense as we read without clearly understanding it or how it works in the text.

Lawrence's belief in this conflict between our natural and social selves also has an effect on how he writes. He needs to find new ways of exploring the deep inner recesses of human personality, those inner drives and compulsions where we are all much the same, rather that those outer, more superficial aspects of our characters, created by social training, where we are all different. It is the latter that most novelists are interested in. This explains why Lawrence's style is so unusual. These new demands require new techniques, new ways of writing as well as new kinds of plot. Each novel of Lawrence's has its own unique features, but it takes the form it does in order to express his evolving thought about the individual's place, or lack of place, in society. Once you have grasped this essential principle of organisation, you have a framework to fit everything else into. But I am anticipating what I hope the rest of this book will demonstrate.

At this point it may help if I outline the method I have adopted in this book. Each chapter begins with a *basic analysis* of the novel in question. Because, crudely, novels tell stories about people, the best entry into a novel is to examine *the plot.* In turn this will lead to a closer investigation of the *main characters,* their needs, hopes and problems. This is most efficiently done by choosing a few short passages featuring them and then asking ourselves some simple questions. In the chapters dealing with the major novels, I have then gone on to consider some *aspects of the novel.* This involves an examination of the society or outer world that the major characters attempt, and usually fail, to fit into. Inevitably, this leads into a consideration of Lawrence's technique, the shape, structure, symbolic and narrative organisation of each fiction, its language, and other aspects of the novelist's craft.

The best way to see how the method works is to look at the

steps in the following chapters and see how the method is applied. Then you can use it for yourself if you want. I have decided to begin, however, by looking at one of Lawrence's short novels. This is a text you can read quickly and which will give you a very clear insight into the concerns and patterns of Lawrence's fiction. That is how I intend to use it, as a way of introducing Lawrence's ideas and just touching on the steps you can use in your critical method. The steps themselves will become much more evident in the chapters that follow on *Sons and Lovers, The Rainbow* and *Women in Love*. These novels all explore Lawrence's sense of the tragic disparity between individual need and society's demands. They are generally accepted as Lawrence's most successful and most important achievement as a novelist. After them comes a chapter on *Lady Chatterley's Lover*, Lawrence's last and most controversial novel, which returns to the industrial Midland setting of his childhood and youth for a final, qualified statement of hope for the individual in the modern world. Finally, at the end of the book, there, is a chapter to help you with writing essays and tackling exam answers.

2

Getting started: a basic analysis of *The Fox* (1923)

The Fox was first published in the American literary magazine *The Dial* in 1922, and in book form with two other short novels a year later. It is a remarkable tale written when Lawrence was at the height of his powers. Because it is short and accessible, I have chosen it as a starting-point for our discussion of Lawrence. I shall use it to examine his ideas and as a basis for exploring the nature of his imagination. You can probably read *The Fox* at a single sitting and this is what I recommend that you do. The first step in any basis analysis is to get a sense of the narrative sequence of events. You have to ask yourself, 'What is happening here?' By working this out, however imperfectly, you are already beginning to construct a response that is more than merely reproducing the story. This is because in your own retelling you are forced to make decisions about what is essential and what is less important. By being selective in this way, you are already shaping a 'critical' understanding of the pattern in the text. Of course, this is only provisional; with rereading and further thought you will almost certainly be forced to amend and adapt it. But you have made a start and that is the important thing. With a long and complex novel, this can be a fairly demanding task in itself and raise all kinds of awkward problems. But with a shorter narrative such as *The Fox* this first step should not prove to difficult.

1 *After reading the novel, think about the story and what kind of pattern you can see in the text.*

This is my version of events:

At the end of the First World War two young spinsters are attempting, rather unsuccessfully, to run an isolated farm in

Berkshire while seeking domestic happiness together. One of the women, Ellen March, is rather 'mannish' and physically vigorous: she does the work around the farm. The other, Jill Banford, is rather delicate and sickly. In particular their efforts at self-sufficiency are being frustrated by a dog fox which keeps killing their chickens.

One night, a young soldier, Henry Grenfel, visits them expecting to find his grandfather, the previous owner of the farm. He is made welcome by Banford, the new owner, and invited to spend his leave on the farm. At first all goes well. Grenfel makes himself useful about the place; indeed he eventually shoots the fox that has been such a nuisance. However, relationships become strained when he begins to woo March: Banford is jealous and greatly distressed. He persists, nevertheless, and eventually March agrees to marry him, but she immediately revokes her acceptance by letter after he returns to camp. Deeply frustrated and furious with Banford, Grenfel manages to get a special twenty-four hour pass and returns to the farm, where, partly by accident and partly by inspired design, he kills Banford in a tree-felling episode. He and March get married and plan to leave for a new life in Canada, but a sense of unease and unresolved struggle persists between them.

What can I make of this? Well, in the broadest terms, the pattern I can see here is one of struggle and conflict between nature and society; or, to focus it rather more sharply, between instinctive desires of an anti-social kind and those institutions of a domestic, civilising nature that most of us endeavour to maintain. March and Banford's relationship is not exactly 'normal' family life and is clearly seen as vulnerable on that account, but they are working for domestic happiness together in a civilised context. Their efforts are frustrated first by natural agencies outside the home, and secondly – and more damagingly – by human agencies within it. What of Lawrence's attitude to all this? Well, frankly, I am not at all sure; he doesn't give too many clues. There are times when he seems to be siding with Grenfel against Banford, but the overall effect is ambiguous. The ending does not give me a sense of happy resolution. One set of problems has been substituted for another, that is all.

Then there's the title. The importance of, and focus on, the fox that Lawrence clearly intends by the title is not self-evident from my synopsis; the farmyard predator is killed halfway through the story. Still I have no doubt that the dominating image of the fox is significant in ways that a recapitulation of the narrative alone cannot capture. Clearly Henry is associated with the fox; both are 'raiders' of domestic peace and natural predators. Yet is Henry *the* fox of the title? If he is, why does he kill the real fox? What significance should we read into that? I do not expect easy answers to these questions, but what I think is becoming clear is that I am engaging with some important problems and asking the right kind of questions.

As I read over my account I am also made aware of how much of the tale's substance has been left out. By concentrating on exterior events – the situation of the spinsters, the arrival of the soldier, his departure, sudden return, and the death of Banford – I have focused on either end of the narrative at the expense of what I obscurely feel is the core of this tale, namely the emotional turmoil and psychological struggle within the characters. This is necessarily masked or hidden by any straightforward narrative account. It is only when we think about the characters that we gain a clearer sense of what an 'interior' novelist Lawrence is for most of the time.

One thing I am quite certain about, however. By retelling the story in this way it becomes evident to me that March is the central figure in this tale. She has the greatest involvement with the fox: Banford stays indoors and Henry, the hunter, merely shoots it as a pest. Moreover, it is she who feels the tug of conflicting loyalties and has to undergo most change. *The Fox* is her story and the best way forward will be to explore her character more fully. I am confident that the more I know about her the better grasp I shall have on the tale as a whole, so I am ready now to move on to the next step.

2 *Select a short passage featuring one of the main characters and try to build upon the ideas you have established so far*

I need to select a passage near the beginning, so I have chosen Lawrence's first detailed description of March, about a page into the text (page references to *The Fox* relate to the Penguin text in *D. H. Lawrence: Three Novellas*, 1960).

> March did most of the outdoor work. When she was out and about, in her puttees and breeches, her belted coat and her loose cap, she looked almost like some graceful, loose-balanced young man, for her shoulders were straight, and her movements easy and confident, even tinged with a little indifference or irony. But her face was not a man's face, ever. The wisps of her crisp dark hair blew about her as she stooped, her eyes were big and wide and dark, when she looked up again, strange, startled, shy and sardonic at once. Her mouth, too, was almost pinched as if in pain and irony. There was something odd and unexplained about her. She would stand balanced on one hip, looking at the fowls pattering about in the obnoxious fine mud of the sloping yard, and calling to her favourite white hen, which came in answer to her name. But there was an almost satirical flicker in March's big, dark eyes as she looked at her three-toed flock pottering about under her gaze, and the same slight dangerous satire in her voice as she spoke to the favoured Patty, who pecked at March's boot by way of friendly demonstration. (p. 86)

It is not at all easy to marshal your thoughts and make a critical analysis of a piece of writing such as this. I shall be giving you more detailed advice on this in the next chapter. For the moment, I am just going to suggest that any piece of imaginative writing involves conflicts or tensions of one sort or another. It might be between the main characters and their society, or between characters, or within characters. It might be between the details of a description, or, more subtly, it might be revealed in the writer's method of presenting the material: what is put into a passage and what is left out. In other words, a conflict is revealed in the writer. Without conflict there can be no story or narrative interest; without tensions of some sort there can be no psychological curiosity to involve the reader in the text. Conflicts or tensions, once identified, can be seen to pervade a work at all levels and you can provide evidence for them on every page. Once spotted, they are the quickest and most effective way of getting into a text and making some sense of it. So what conflicts or tensions can we discern in this, our first close view of March?

Well, we have learnt that Banford is 'a small, thin, delicate thing with spectacles' (p. 85) and, in contrast, March is clearly associated with the practical day-to-day running of the farm. In consequence, she has assumed a male role in work and dress. I would say that this adopted male persona does not fully satisfy March or fit the complexity of her character. This seems to be one source of tension in the passage and, I suspect, may be a key element to bear in mind as the story evolves. I can also see that the second half of the passage takes up that sense of a conflict between people and nature that I have already noted as a general feature of this tale.

I now need to follow up these speculations by close work on the substance of the text that will either provide supporting evidence or force me to modify my views. Lawrence writes that there is something 'odd and unexplained' about March. From a distance she looks 'almost like' a young man in her male clothes, but as we move closer we can see that her face could never be a man's face, 'ever'. Her 'straight' shoulders and 'easy and confident' movements are contrasted and seem to conflict with the 'wisps' of dark hair and the big, dark startled eyes. Lawrence pays particular attention to March's eyes and mouth. It is here that unresolved tensions seem to declare themselves most fully. The eyes are 'shy and sardonic', the mouth 'almost pinched as if in pain and irony'. Lawence, as exterior narrator, is fastening here on physical details that seem to betray inner states of mind or feeling, but he leaves the question open and unresolved. We simply do not know why March should be both shy and sardonic or why she might be in a state of self-depreciating suffering. There is just a sense of someone not living in full accord with herself. Similarly, when Lawrence moves away again to view March in the farmyard, we do not know why she should look at or address the chickens in a satirical manner.

The story has only just begun, but the last part of the paragraph becomes more meaningful when we consider it in context. It is clear from the opening that the girls are hopeless farmers. Their rather woolly idealism, their social desires and aspirations, are set against the stubborn intransigence of nature. March seems to recognise something of their folly as she tends her chickens here. At least, that is how I would interpret the 'satirical flicker' in her eyes and the 'dangerous satire' in her voice. You may feel differently. I do get the sense, too, of an unbridgeable gap and a clash of interests between people and nature in which nature is not going to be bested. Patty, the favourite chicken, may be addressed satirically, but she, in turn, gives March a peck at her boot, 'by way of friendly demonstration'.

I feel I have made some progress with March's character. I have spotted a tension in her, but I have also got a sense that her interior conflict is, in some way, related to an outer one between people and nature; I am not sure how and I need to explore further. I think my best move will be to take another look at March at some point of crucial development.

3 *Select a second passage for discussion*

> The trees on the wood-edge were darkish, brownish green in the full light – for it was the end of August. Beyond, the naked, copper-like shafts and limbs of the pine trees shone in the air. Nearer the rough grass, with its long, brownish stalks all agleam, was full of light. The fowls were round about – the ducks were still swimming on the pond under the pine trees. March looked at it all, saw it all, and did not see it. She heard Banford speaking to the fowls in the distance – and she did not hear. What was she thinking about? Heaven knows. Her consciousness was, as it were, held back.
>
> She lowered her eyes, and suddenly saw the fox. He was looking up at her. Her chin was pressed down, and his eyes were looking up. They met her eyes. And he knew her. She was spellbound – she knew he knew her. So he looked into her eyes, and her soul failed her. He knew her, he was not daunted.
>
> She struggled, confusedly she came to herself, and saw him making off, with slow leaps over some fallen boughs, slow impudent jumps. Then he glanced over his shoulder, and ran smoothly away. She saw his brush held smooth like a feather, she saw his white buttocks twinkle. And he was gone, soft as the wind. (pp. 88–9)

Actually, this passage isn't much further on but it did seem to select itself; March's first encounter with the fox is clearly crucial both for the subsequent development of her own character and for the story as a whole.

Obviously the crucial opposition here is between the human world and the natural world as epitomised in March's confrontation with the fox. In the first passage we looked at March from the outside. Now Lawrence has shifted his point of view and moved us inside her consciousness. This is particularly true in the first paragraph. Thereafter we seem to move around quite a bit. Sometimes we are seeing things from the outside, sometimes from March's point of view – and sometimes even from the fox's. Once we are alerted to this mobility of viewpoint, we can see it as a constant feature of Lawrence's style as an imaginative writer: it adds greatly to the drama and sense of immediacy that his writing always has.

Registered through March's consciousness, the first paragraph gives us a scene of harmony and tranquillity. We seem to be in an ideal world where people and nature are at one. Nature is undoubtedly and palpably present; our sense of an outside world is built up by a number of accurately obscured details. It is the end of the summer, so the leaves on the trees are 'darkish, brownish green'. The texture of the grass is 'rough' with 'long, brownish stalks'. The work of the farm goes on, ducks swim on the pond, Banford speaks to the fowls, yet there is also a mesmerising, hallucinatory quality about the scene. The shafts and limbs of the pine trees 'shine copper-like' in the dark, and the grass is 'agleam' and 'full of light'. This tension in levels of perception – one external, the other more subjective – is a source of potential conflict reconciled within March herself. She hears but does not hear, sees but does not see. From the beginning we have been made aware that she lives in a divided, trance-like state of mind, as if her social being were something apart from her inner self. The final sentence of the first paragraph quoted emphasises this: 'Her consciousness was, as it were, held back.'

The fox breaks into this reverie, forcing itself brutally into March's consciousness. The fox is not a dream and cannot be accommodated into any harmonious, tranquil, idealised world. March meets the eye of the fox and is 'known' by him. Exactly what Lawrence means by this, or by saying that March's 'soul' failed her, just isn't clear but it is obviously important. Maybe the fox represents some truth about the world (or about herself?) that March cannot fully admit and acknowledge consciously. The repetition of 'knew' in a number of short, emphatic, simple sentences heightens the drama of the exchange in the second paragraph. The syntax and the impersonal use of pronouns emphasise the conflict of wills between the woman and the animal in which the woman is mastered. 'She lowered her eyes . . . . He was looking up . . . . Her chin was pressed down . . . his eyes were looking up. . . . He knew her. . . . she knew he knew her. . . . He knew her, he was not daunted.' This kind of parallelism, repetition and simple insistence is in marked contrast to the loose casualness of the preceding descriptive paragraph.

I may be uncertain what exactly Lawrence means to signify by the fox, but, whatever else it means or is, the fox is a real fox. We, along with March, are forced to acknowledge this in the next paragraph when, moving away from the moment of 'knowledge', we see the fox escaping in cinematic slow motion.

The writing becomes lyrical with the repetition of 'slow', 'smooth' and 'soft', as Lawrence celebrates the fox's going, the slow leaps, the smooth brush held 'like a feather' and the twinkling white buttocks, with a kind of reverence for the animal's essential nature.

So far ı have concentrated on March to the exclusion of the other characters. I think it is time to broaden the discusion by examining her in a social context.

4 *Select a third passage for discussion*

> Tonight, however, he took a Captain Mayne Reid book from Banford's shelf and sat down with knees wide apart and immersed himself in his story. His brownish fair hair was long, and lay on his head like a thick cap, combed sideways. He was still in his shirt-sleeves, and bending forward under the lamp-light, with his knees stuck wide apart and the book in his hand and his whole figure absorbed in the rather strenuous business of reading, he gave Banford's sitting-room the look of a lumber camp. She resented this. For on her sitting-room floor she had a red Turkey rug and dark stain round, the fire place had fashionable green tiles, the piano stood open with the latest dance music: she played quite well: and on the walls were March's hand-painted swans and water lilies. Moreover, with the logs nicely, tremulously burning in the grate, the thick curtains drawn, the doors all shut, and the pine trees hissing and shuddering in the wind outside, it was cosy, it was refined and nice. She resented the big, long-legged youth sticking his khaki knees out and sitting there with his soldier's shirt-cuffs buttoned on his thick red wrists. From time to time he turned a page, and from time to time he gave a sharp look at the fire, settling the logs. Then he immersed himself again in the intense and isolated business of reading.
>
> March, on the far side of the table, was spasmodically crocheting. Her mouth was pursed in an odd way, as when she had dreamed the fox's brush burned it, her beautiful, crisp black hair strayed in wisps. But her whole figure was absorbed in its bearing, as if she herself was miles away. In a sort of semi-dream she seemed to be hearing the fox singing round the house in the wind, singing wildly and sweetly and like a madness. With red but well-shaped hands she slowly crocheted the white cotton, very slowly, awkwardly. (pp.109–10)

By the time we reach this passage the story has progressed significantly. Henry Grenfel has arrived and made his presence felt, especially in his wooing of March. Banford does not yet know this, but she senses a rival and tensions have begun to surface. What we appear to have here is a tranquil scene of domestic contentment with the three characters quietly involved in their respective tasks; what Lawrence reveals is a whole complex of emotions within the characters that no ordinary onlooker could deduce from this silent scene. Henry, at this stage in the evening absorbed in his book, provides the unwitting focus for Banford's resentment, and March's strange reverie. In the first paragraph, we see Henry from Banford's point of view and our view of him is coloured by her social and class prejudices. In the second paragraph, we move over to March and enter her mind. The tension that Lawrence expresses here is more psychological as he explores her divided consciousness. She is apparently occupied with her crocheting inside the house, but her thoughts are outside with her 'dream fox'.

Many of the details in the passage, pick up this persistent tension in *The Fox* between an outdoor world that is dangerous, threatening but, for March at least, rather exciting too, and a more comforting and secure, domestic situation. Henry reads an old-fashioned adventure yarn, and belongs to that male world of hunting, soldiering and adventure. He brings 'the look of a lumber-camp' into Banford's cosy sitting-room with its middle-class comforts and culture: the red Turkey rug, the 'fashionable green tiles', the hand-printed ornaments and the piano with the latest dance music. We know we are seeing these things from Banford's point of view by the manner in which the scene is described; the logs 'nicely, tremulously burning', the curtains drawn, the door shut against the stormy night, all give an air of complacency. As Banford thinks to herself, 'It was cosy, it was refined and nice.' Henry brings a coarser, male, outdoor world into this precious, hot-house atmosphere. His hair is 'like a thick cap', he is in his shirt-sleeves and even the activity of reading is 'a strenuous business' to him. The references to his khaki uniform, his lack of social elegance and his 'thick red wrists' are all indications of Banford's growing distaste for this working-class soldier.

In a more secretive, interior manner, March is also uncommitted to the domesticity of the scene. Her crocheting is 'spasmodic' and, rather like Henry's reading, it is 'slow and awkward'. Though her hands are well shaped, like Henry's wrists they are 'red'; they are more used to outdoor work. Henry is indoors but absorbed in a tale of outdoor adventure. Though nominally inside, March is even less aware of her immediate surroundings; she is 'miles away' in a 'semi-dream' listening to the wild singing of the fox. Only Banford's consciousness remains consistently within the room itself.

I have talked about Lawrence's trick of fastening onto outward mannerisms that reveal states of mind. This is very evident here. Henry's wide-kneed, casual posture reveals his rather contemptuous male arrogance. I may not be particularly sympathetic to Banford, but I sense that she is right to feel hostile. Henry does threaten her standards and values. As the text progresses, March's pursed mouth has become a repeated image associated with her self-doubt and mental pain that gathers resonance and significance. On the night of Henry's arrival, March had an extraordinary dream. She dreamt that a singing yellow fox lured her into the darkness outside the house, bit her and burned her mouth with his brush. It is this dream that is referred to in the present passage, so the pursed mouth is now associated with the power of the fox. At first the fox was a real fox that stole chickens; now it has become much more. It is a 'dream fox' that is obsessing March, taking over her inner life and becoming a focus for her dissatisfactions. The idea of a fox singing 'wildly and sweetly and like a madness' is a disturbing one. In my mind it makes March's 'dream fox' akin to the sirens that lured men to their destruction. In any event, it is a surreal image and belongs to a different order of reality from the crochet, the red Turkey rug and the 'hand-painted swans'. There is not much in March's outward behaviour to suggest a particularly imaginative personality, so this aspect of her character interests me and I should like to explore it further.

5 *Select a fourth passage for discussion*

> That night March had another dream. She dreamed that Banford was dead, and that she, March, was sobbing her heart out. Then she had to put Banford into her coffin. And the coffin was the rough wood-box in which the bits of chopped wood were kept in the kitchen, by the fire. This was the coffin, and there was no other, and March was in agony and dazed bewilderment, looking for something to line the box with, something to make if soft with, something to cover up the poor, dead darling. Because she couldn't lay her in there just in her white, thin nightdress, in the horrible wood-box. So she hunted and hunted, and picked up thing after thing, and threw it aside in the agony of dream-frustration. And in her dream-despair all she could

> find that would do was a fox-skin. She knew that it wasn't right, that this was not what she should have. But it was all she could find. And so she folded the brush of the fox, and laid her darling Jill's head on this, and she brought round the skin of the fox and laid it on the top of the body, so that it seemed to make a whole ruddy, fiery coverlet, and she cried and cried, and woke to find the tears streaming down her face. (pp. 123–4)

This is March's second dream on the night that Henry shoots the fox. By this stage Banford knows about Henry's proposal and March's acceptance. The dream seems to express March's mixed feelings about Banford.

We are right inside March's interior consciousness here. The censors of social identity and day-time reality have been removed and the passage is very nakedly emotional and direct. Vulnerable aspects in March's personality are exposed in a way she cannot allow or finds difficult to express in her daily life. Because we are in a 'dream reality', any tensions are 'dream tensions', not logical or consistent with common sense. The dream expresses March's fears and resentments, guilt and pity, over her relationship with Henry and its effect on Banford. In the way of dreams, these are all mixed up with the dead fox so recently held up by Henry outside their window in the middle of the night.

March has to bury Banford. Banford is dead like the fox. By association, this seems to suggest that Banford too has been killed by Henry, or, rather, that March wishes that she had been. She wishes Banford dead but she also wants her laid to rest appropriately. The wood-box coffin and the chopped wood also suggest Henry. He was sawing wood in the shed when he proposed to March. The chopped wood also suggests the final felling of the dead tree that does, in fact, kill Banford. Dreams, in literature as in life, can be a mode of prophecy. In the first dream the fox burned her mouth anticipating the effect of Henry's first kiss.

There's no doubting the extremity of March's feelings. In her 'dream frustration' and 'dream despair' she 'sobs her heart out' in 'agony and dazed bewilderment'. There's no doubt of her concern for Banford, 'the poor, dead darling', and of the need to make her comfortable. The use of the fox skin is highly problematic; it seems right and somehow meaningful but I am hard put to *explain* the meaning. Any version would be my version, personal to me, not necessarily right for you. The fox pelt is beautiful and vital:

it keeps Banford warm; it protects her from the hardness of the horrible box; it is more adequate than Banford's own 'white, thin nightdress' but it 'wasn't right'. It is all that March can find, but it is not what Banford should have. This implies by deplacement of image and association that Banford is going to share the fate of the fox. March wants her dead but cannot acknowledge it openly. She wants her out of her life but does not want her to suffer. The rich warmth of the pelt and the manner in which it is lovingly wrapped around the dead body is profoundly ambiguous. It implies care and concern but also the victory of the fox, or what it stands for. It metaphorically consumes Banford as if by fire – it is a 'ruddy, fiery coverlet' – and buries her.

What we are seeing in this passage is Lawrence's capacity as a writer to explore those moods, intuitions, instincts, areas of consciousness that lie just below what may be consciously grasped or formulated. March herself, we feel, would be hard put to express her own emotions. Think of her letter to Henry, full of clichés and trite phrases. Lawrence has created a character of few words and apparently limited emotional range who yet is capable of deep feelings. He is able to open up March's complex emotional life, express her feelings for her through image and symbol, in a manner that is totally convincing and compelling. It is one of his major, distinctive skills as a writer.

6 *Have I achieved a sufficiently complex sense of the novel?*

My primary task in working towards a basic analysis of this tale was to get a better understanding of March's character. If working through a selected number of short passages has brought me to a realisation of just how subtle Lawrence's characterisation is, that is all to the good. However many passages I examine, though, I shall never 'know' Ellen March, if only for the simple reason that she does not 'know' herself. One of Lawrence's distinctive abilities as an imaginative writer is to show how inadequate and untenable any notions of 'character' as something stable, fixed and 'knowable' are. To understand this is to take a big step forward in our study of Lawrence.

Still, there has to come a point in your initial examination of a text when you must stop and take stock, look over what you have done, try to summarise and see where you have to go next. I could go on looking at passages indefinitely, but time is limited and there is a real danger that you will begin to lose sight of the big points by becoming obsessed with small details. The art of criticism is the art of selection; you have to learn what must go in and what can be left out.

I said at the beginning that a mere narrative account of the tale's happenings would not get us into the substance of the tale, which is the struggle and conflict within characters. By taking a careful look at March, however, I think I have made some progress in exposing those inner tensions and how Lawrence builds his text up from them. March is a divided being; Banford and Henry seek to possess her through one aspect of her personality at the expense and exclusion of the other. I should need to support this by more detailed study, but I have a sense that Banford is an indoor sort of person, genteel, kindly but also rather weak and spiteful. She seems to draw out the caring, dominant and protective side of March's nature. In contrast, Henry is the outdoor type, physically strong and a bit wild, certainly instinctively sexual. Almost against her will and better judgement, March is drawn by his physical magnetism. Like the fox, he 'knows' her and she is 'spellbound' in his presence. Certainly he forces her to confront the inadequacy and the unmet needs in her present way of life.

What about the fox, its power as a symbol and its relationship to the three main characters? I have some ideas but I should like to develop them further. In particular I should like a closer look at Henry as he is most closely associated with the fox. To do this I shall examine a passage from the final confrontation between Henry and Banford, which forms the crisis of the narrative.

> Henry looked up at her, and met her queer, round-pupilled, weak eyes staring behind her spectacles. He was perfectly still. He looked away, up at the weak, leaning tree. And as he looked into the sky, like a huntsman who is watching a flying bird, he thought to himself: 'If the tree falls in just such a way, and spins just so much as it falls, then the branch there will strike her exactly as she stands on top of that bank.'
>
> He looked at her again. She was wiping the hair from her brow again, with that perpetual gesture. In his heart he had decided her death. A terrible still force seemed in him, and a power that was just his. If he turned even a hair's breadth in the wrong direction, he would lose the power.
>
> 'Mind yourself, Miss Banford,' he said. And his heart held perfectly still, in the terrible pure will that she should not move.

> 'Who, me, mind myself?' she cried, her father's jeering tone in her voice. 'Why, do you think you might hit me with the axe?'
>
> 'No, it's just possible the tree might, though,' he answered soberly. But the tone of his voice seemed to her to imply that he was only being falsely solicitous, and trying to make her move because it was his will to move her. (p. 151)

Henry and Banford are natural adversaries and this is the final battle of will between them. Henry has returned to the farm in a terrible rage against Banford because he holds her responsible for March's change of heart about their marriage. He arrives to find March struggling to cut down a dead tree. As he prepares to finish the job himself, he warns Banford of the dangers of standing too close. The tension in the passage is between what Henry says as a socially responsible individual and what he wills as a hunter resolved on Banford's death. It's a dramatic scene: there is the external conflict between the two and also the internal drama within Henry himself.

Banford is seen externally from Henry's point of view, thus excluding her from our sympathy; she is a quarry or 'game', akin to the flying duck that a hunter might shoot and similarly subject to his ruthless calculations. She is seen as a rather pathetic creature, 'short-sighted' in more ways than one. Rather like March's pursed mouth, the gesture with her hair has ben established as an external sign of her inner character. We have learnt to associate it with her weakness and her stubbornness. Her jeering tone also establishes her social contempt for this working-class farm boy. Her father, we remember, was a tradesman in Islington. Of course, her retort to Henry's warning reveals her ignorance as well as her sarcasm. It is in marked contrast to Henry's cool calculations. He is doubly clever (as a fox?) by speaking to her in a tone that implies one thing while really meaning another. He is possessed by 'a terrible still force' that takes him over in an almost supernatural sense; he becomes an agent of 'pure' predatory will exerting some hidden, intangible power over her. She is deceived by his 'falsely solicitous' tone and allows her hostility to cloud her judgement. While being told the truth, she remains unaware of the danger she is in.

What of Lawrence's attitude to all this? What I sense here is an alarming challenge to conventional Christian or humanist morality, or any liberal sense of right or wrong. Indeed, there seems to be a suspension of moral judgement altogether, something very unusual in English fiction. In this battle of wills between Banford and Henry there is no room for compromise whatsoever. They represent totally antithetical forces and the victory of one can only be achieved by the total destruction of the other. To what extent Lawrence takes sides in this conflict is a very delicate matter and requires careful reading of the tale as a whole. Many critics have seen this battle of wills as a struggle and eventual victory of life over death. Banford is like a dead tree and has to be removed. Others, more negatively and critically, have seen it more as a triumph of the strong over the weak, again with Lawrence's approval. I am not sure that it is as simple as this but you will have to make up your own mind. Perhaps the reactions of March and the rather open, unresolved nature of the ending are the key to the problem. Note that for March 'something was missing' (p. 153) after Banford's death and she suffers as if physically wounded even after her marriage while Henry remains dissatisfied and thwarted in his victory. Marriage seems not to produce a happy ending but rather a new, painful beginning.

In a sense Henry *is* the fox and March is right to see him as such. But he is not always and consistently so. Symbols are ambiguous; they cannot be pinned down and that is the source of their power. Henry does have finer feelings too and a sense of emotional responsibility towards March. All the characters have social roles as well as passions, but they fit uneasily into them; we sense their instability. For example, Henry is a soldier; soldiers are violent but they also have discipline and preserve order. There is a paradox here that Lawence exploits. Henry can be sensitive and courteous, and one part of him does try to save Banford. The woman are not simple victims either. They seem to connive in their own defeat. Banford will not move, despite the warning, and March searches, seeks out her fox. Her dreams suggest her implications with the fox, too. She and Henry are linked through the animal in a vital, largely unspoken, association that excludes Banford.

Why does Lawrence call his story *The Fox* and what does he mean to signify by it? To my mind – and it is only my opinion – the fox symbolises a kind of life energy that is neither good or evil, just simply there. Beautiful yet cruel, it is ever-present in nature and in us. Our social selves are sometimes powerless to resist this energy; it must find its expression through us, whatever the consequences, and this is most apparent in our sexual needs. Whether or not we should resist it is not Lawrence's concern. This is what makes *The Fox* an unsentimental love story of such a new and radically challenging kind.

In conclusion, let us try to summarise our findings about Lawrence based on our study of this tale. I think this is worth doing because the patterns and concerns we find here are likely to be characteristic of any Lawrence novel that you read. I have said that all fictions have conflicts and tensions in them, but those in *The Fox* are particularly violent. Nature and society are constantly at war with each other and, because individuals are necessarily part-natural, part-social, they are torn apart by this conflict too. Lawrence needs to show the stresses and strains within people and the difficulties they have in maintaining relationships with each other. He makes us aware of the complexity, but also the instability, of our identities – how easily we can be thrown into confusion. Extremes of love and hate are of particular interest to Lawrence because, as happens here, they overturn reason and restraint. He is very alert to the ambiguity in strong emotions and expresses this in a language that seems often obscure or theatrically excessive.

Because Lawrence is so aware of the wild and passionate in people, you might feel he has gone too far in his rejections of ordinary humdrum living and the disciplines of normal, social life. There does not seem much moral control in Lawrence in ways that we can easily appreciate, yet the poetry in his writing can be very persuasive. As readers we are sometimes made to realise that the complacencies of received social wisdom do not always measure up to the challenges, the needs, the raw pain, of being alive. Reading Lawrence can be exhausting, but it is also a very exhilarating business. With these thoughts in mind, we can move on to his first major novel.

3

Sons and Lovers (1913)

I Constructing an overall analysis

THE PRIMARY purpose of any novel is to tell a story that entertains us or compels our interest in some way. This is an obvious thing to say, yet it can easily be forgotten when you have to study a lengthy piece of fiction for essays or exams. The best way into a big novel such as *Sons and Lovers* is to read it briskly so as to get some sense of the shape of the narrative and to find out what it is about. You are then ready to take the first step in shaping a critical understanding of the novel.

1 *After reading the novel, think about the story and what kind of pattern you can see in the text*

This is my version of events:

> During the second half of the nineteenth century, Gertrude Coppard, a proud serious girl of cultured background but no wealth, marries a young miner, Walter Morel, and lives with him in Bestwood, a Midland mining village. The marriage is not a success, as the difference of background proves an insurmountable barrier to communication and mutual trust. As Walter becomes increasingly bitter and rejected, so Gertrude seeks consolation in her sons, in whom she rests her middle-class aspirations. William, her eldest son, moves to London and seems destined to achieve success but dies tragically young from an illness brought on by stress and overwork. Mrs Morel focuses all her love and moral energy on Paul, her second son. Paul similarly achieves some emancipation from the mining community by becoming a spiral overseer in a Nottingham hosiery

factory and, in his spare time, a promising designer and artist. However, such professional and social emancipation is not matched by any corresponding psychological growth to maturity, for Paul feels bound by ties of love and loyalty to his mother in a way that inhibits full relationships with other women. His intense friendship with Miriam, the daughter of a local farmer, and later a passionate affair with Clara, a Nottingham woman separated from her husband, both fail to bring enduring satisfaction while his mother lives and needs him. He rejects them both. Finally, his mother dies after a prolonged and painful illness, leaving Paul bereft and alone, uncertain whether he has the will to go on living.

What can I make of the story at this general level? Well, although it is a while before this becomes clear, it is evident that this is Paul Morel's story. It follows his growth and development from infancy to young manhood. The narrative becomes increasingly shaped to his life. Whatever else there is to the book, I can say with confidence that *Sons and Lovers* is an unusual version of a common form of novel – namely, the 'education' novel, where the focus is on the growth to maturity of a young person. *Sons and Lovers* is unusual in that Paul does not appear to have learned much about himself by the end of the book. You may feel that this is rather an obvious point to make, but you shouldn't be afraid of stating the obvious. It is by dwelling on the implications of such generalities that you can work your way into a novel.

As we are considering the obvious, it is always worth examining a novel's title. It follows from what I have said that the novel should be called 'Paul Morel', but it isn't, though in early draft form it was. Why did Lawrence change his mind? In the final title he is shifting the emphasis away from Paul, instead he is drawing our attention to a set of relationships – in fact, two sets of relationships: one ('sons') within the family and another ('lovers') outside the family. Some connection seems to be implied between the two. By using such a title, Lawrence is emphasising a connection between men's capacity to form serious adult relationships and their first relationship with their parents. It is also evident from my first reading that the distinction between 'sons' and 'lovers' is blurred; Paul is a son and a lover, so, although the novel tends to focus more and more on Paul Morel, his problems, his needs and his growth, the family context and in particular the relationship with his mother is never allowed to fade or recede too far. Moreover, the plural form of the title reminds me that, although clearly the most important, Paul is one of three sons. Again this emphasises Lawrence's insistence that we read the novel as a story of a family and not just Paul's story. This is confirmed by casting an eye over the contents page. It is evident from the chapter headings that Part I is family-oriented and ends with the death of William. It is only in Part II that Paul's concerns become dominant.

Having completed these general procedures, we need to get to grips with the text itself. It is comparatively easy to chat about novels in a general way as if the characters were real and the events were real life; it is much harder to think of them as texts made up of words. The sheer size of a novel can be very intimidating and, if we are to make any progress, we need to break it down into some of its constituent elements and so make it more manageable. By making the text more manageable in this way we reduce the scale of the task but we also force ourselves to focus on detail. Gradually these details will build up to give our more general discussion sharpness and reference. The usual and most obvious way to start this process, as we saw when looking at *The Fox*, is by choosing an important character in a dramatic or tense situation early in the novel and to discuss a passage in detail. So, after getting a general sense of the narrative, the next stage is

2 *Select a short passage featuring one of the main characters and try to build upon the ideas you have established so far*

The novel begins by examining the relationship between Gertrude and Walter Morel, their backgrounds, courtship and early married life. A good place to start is by looking at a passage early in the novel that focuses on the conflict that we know characterises their relationship. Here is such a passage that occurs midway through the first chapter (page references to the novel relate to the Penguin edition, 1981):

> William was only one year old, and his mother was proud of him, he was so pretty. She was not well off now, but her sisters kept the boy in clothes. Then, with his little white hat curled with an ostrich feather, and his white coat, he was a joy to her, the twining wisps of hair clustering round his head. Mrs Morel lay listening, one Sunday morning, to the chatter of the father and child downstairs. Then she

> dozed off. When she came downstairs, a great fire glowed in the grate, the room was hot, the breakfast was roughly laid, and seated in his armchair, against the chimney-piece, sat Morel, rather timid; and standing between his legs, the child – cropped like a sheep, with such an odd round poll – looking, wondering at her; and on a newspaper spread out upon the hearth rug, a myriad of crescent-shaped curls, like the petals of a marigold scattered in the reddening firelight.
>
> Mrs Morel stood still. It was her first baby. She went very white, and was unable to speak.
>
> 'What dost think o' 'im?' Morel laughed uneasily.
>
> She gripped her two fists, lifted them, and came forward. Morel shrank back.
>
> 'I could kill you, I could!' she said. She choked with rage, her two fists uplifted.
>
> 'Yer non want ter make a wench on 'im,' Morel said, in a frightened tone, bending his head to shield his eyes from hers. His attempt at laughter had vanished.
>
> The mother looked down at the jagged, close-clipped head of her child. She put her hands on his hair, and stroked and fondled his head.
>
> 'Oh – my boy!' she faltered. Her lips trembled, her face broke, and, snatching up the child, she buried her face in his shoulder and cried painfully. She was one of those women who cannot cry; whom it hurts as it hurts a man. It was like ripping something out of her, her sobbing.
>
> Morel sat with his elbows on his knees, his hands griped together till the knuckles were white. He gazed in the fire, feeling almost stunned, as if he could not breathe. (pp. 50–1)

When confronted by a passage such as this, it is often difficult to know where to begin. In Chapter 2 we were concentrating on Lawrence's ideas and just getting a sense of what kind of writer he is. Although I did build up my basic analysis in stages and looked as passages quite closely, I kept my method secret and just asked you to think about conflict and tension in the text. In this chapter I shall be more concerned with method and especially how you should tackle a passage on your own. This task is less formidable if you follow an orderly sequence that enables you analyse a passage in a systematic manner. Here is such a sequence.

(a) *Make a short statement of what the passage is about.*
(b) *Search for an opposition or tension within the passage.*
(c) *Analyse the details of the passage, relating them to the opposition already noted.*
(d) *Try to say how the passage relates to the novel as a whole.*

(e) *Search for anything distinctive about the passage, particularly in the area of style, which you have not already noted.*

Following a number of steps like this will force you to break a passage down and focus on its details. Depending on the passage you choose, not all the steps will have equal relevance, but they will help you organise your response and make it harder for you to miss important points. This will become clearer if we systematically apply the method to the above passage from *Sons and Lovers*.

(a) *Make a short statement of what the passage is about.* This passage is about the first major conflict in the Morels' marriage. Walter attempts to assert his authority by cutting William's hair, as he considers his wife is pampering the child and making him effeminate.

(b) *Search for an opposition or tension within the passage.* The passage illustrates the battle between husband and wife, based on their difference of social class, that is going to dominate the first part of the novel. They differ as regards both their own needs and their demands for their children.

(c) *Analyse the details of the passage, relating them to the opposition already noted.* William's white coat and hat with its ostrich feather, his 'twining wisps of hair' are an expression of Gertrude Morel's middle-class fantasy. This is supported by family charity and is ridiculously inappropriate to the rough domesticity of a miner's cottage interior that we see here, with the great fire burning, the breakfast roughly laid, the newspaper on the hearth rug. These details provide the setting for Mrs Morel's cruel awakening to the realities of her situation. William's cropped head is a brutal expression of her disillusionment; her dreams are shorn but are still seen as beautiful in the evocative simile of the cropped curls as the petals of a marigold. An interesting complication in the way Lawrence describes this conflict is the manner in which both parents react. It is the cultured, religious Mrs Morel who breaks into an elemental rage and grief. In contrast, Walter is alarmed, defensive and finally 'stunned' into passivity by her response to his clumsy act. Thus Lawrence reveals how fragile our class and gender roles can be at times of emotional crisis.

(d) *Try to say how the passage relates to the novel as a whole.* This is one of several passages I could have chosen to demonstrate the clash of values and expectations between Mr and Mrs Morel. From the beginning the children are seen as victims. Already Mrs Morel is shown to be the stronger in this battle of wills, while her husband is put onto the defensive and at odds with his own children. He is, though, making an effort as a parent; the fire is made up, the breakfast 'roughly laid', he chatters to his son, yet we are not allowed into his motives as we are into the grief of his wife. There is, after all, some justices in his assertion that William should not be made into a girl; if he is clumsy, his wife is living in a fantasy world that must be destroyed. There is a sense that the narrator is more inclined to favour the mother, as it is her response and consequently her point of view that are dwelt on, but the father's 'stunned' incomprehension still draws our attention and compassion.

(e) *Search for anything distinctive about the passage, particularly in the area of style, which you have not already noted.* Looking at Lawrence's style here alerts me to his interest in the relationship between inner states at feeling and the outward expression of them. There are only four brief utterances, Walter's being appropriately in dialect, but Lawence gives a lot of attention to what's going on inside the characters, to the complex emotions that they are unable to express. He does this by showing us the outward signs of emotions, whether they be tone, gesture or description. The second part of the passage is full of these indications. Morel laughs 'uneasily', speaks 'in a frightened tone', averts his gaze from his wife and finally adopts a frozen posture before the fire, his hands clenched and his knuckles white. She, on her part, goes very white, lifts her fists, chokes with rage, and finally breaks down into 'ripping' sobs, her face buried into her son's shoulder.

I think I've got enough out of the passage now to move on. So the next stage is

3 *Select a second passage for discussion*

Each additional passage you choose should enrich your perception and strengthen your grasp of the novel. Go for memorable scenes that made an impression on your first reading. At this stage it also makes sense to follow the fortunes of the main characters. I have said that *Sons and Lovers* begins as a family study. I have looked at one family scene that has crucial consequences for Mrs Morel and affects her whole subsequent attitude towards her husband. It obviously makes sense if, therefore, I now look at another, later family scene in which Paul, the eventual hero, features, so as to show his relationships with the other family members.

> Paul won a prize in a competition in a child's paper. Everybody was highly jubilant.
>
> 'Now you'd better tell your father when he comes in,' said Mrs Morel. 'You know how he carries on and says he's never told anything.'
>
> 'All right,' said Paul. But he would almost rather have forfeited the prize than have to tell his father.
>
> 'I've won a prize in a competition, Dad,' he said.
>
> Morel turned round to him.
>
> 'Have you, my boy? What sort of a competition?
>
> 'Oh, nothing – about famous women.'
>
> 'And how much is the prize, then, as you've got?'
>
> 'It's a book.'
>
> 'Oh, indeed!'
>
> 'About birds.'
>
> 'Hm – hm!'
>
> And that was all. Conversation was impossible between the father and any other member of the family. He was an outsider. He had denied the God in him.
>
> The only times when he entered again into the life of his own people was when he worked, and was happy at work. Sometimes, in the evening, he cobbled the boots or mended the kettle or his pit-bottle. then he always wanted several attendants, and the children enjoyed it. They united with him in the work, in the actual doing of something, when he was his real self again.
>
> He was a good workman, dexterous, and one who, when he was in a good humour, always sang. He had whole periods, months, almost years, of friction and nasty temper. Then sometimes he was jolly again. It was nice to see him run with a piece of red-hot iron into the scullery, crying:
>
> 'Out of my road – out of my road!' (pp. 102–3)

(a) *Make a short statement of what the passage is about.* This passage shows Walter Morel exiled from the intellectual life of the family. The home is now dominated by the mother's values and the father has no place there except when working about his chores.

(b) *Search for an opposition or tension within the passage.* The opposition within the passage is between Paul and his father, who cannot share language and the values that a command of language brings. In his attempts to discuss the competition and the prize, Morel is not helped by the boy, who is evasive and unforthcoming. Such scenes set the pattern for Paul's relationship, or lack of relationship, with his father for the rest of the novel. There is also a tension between the strained dialogue in the first half of the extract and the full joyous description of Paul's father at work in the two paragraphs that follow. There is tension, then, between speech and action.

(c) *Analyse the details of the passage, relating them to the opposition already noted.* When we look at the details it is evident that the narrator occasionally conspires with the family against the father. The 'everybody' of the second sentence clearly excludes Walter Morel. In his discussion with his father, Paul adopts his mother's assumptions (implied by the phrase 'you'd better tell') that Morel will not be interested. Paul's responses to his father's questions are brief and unhelpful. On his part, Walter can only think of prizes and reward in financial terms; culture, inquiry for its own sake, theoretical knowledge, are alien to him, but, again, he is hardly helped by his son's grudging responses: 'Oh, nothing . . . . It's a book. . . . About birds.'

When Lawrence talks about Morel entering into the life of his 'own people', this is an ambiguous phrase. Does it mean his family or his class? In a sense Morel's family are *not* 'his own people': he is only at home with himself when he brings the world of the pit into the family routine. This is the world of vigorous physical activity interspersed with song and speech which is not abstracted but related to physical action and the task in hand: 'Out of my road – out of my road!' His work needs community, so the children are drawn into it; there is a sense of warmth, bustle, action.

(d) *Try to say how the passage relates to the novel as a whole.* When first reading the novel you were no doubt struck by the violence of Walter Morel, his aggression and unsociability, and you may feel that this passage, which shows him in a better light, is untypical. Yet the positive side of Walter, his enjoyment of simple pleasure – indeed his domesticity, surprisingly enough – is often shown in these early chapters: cooking his breakfast, singing at his chores, mending his gear. Also we are shown his timid attempts to communicate with his wife and Paul, which are always repulsed. The balance between the faults and virtues of Paul's parents is well maintained if we think carefully, and yet that is not our sense as we read the history of their relationship overall. Why?

I think it is because of an imbalance in the narrative commentary best illustrated here by the sentence 'He had denied the God in him,' What exactly does Lawrence mean by 'God' here? I take it to mean when one is integrated as a personality, in harmony with the best in oneself and most completely fulfilled. If this is so, then the second half of the passage refutes the first. In his work Walter Morel is affirming the best in himself. Isn't it rather that sometimes his family deny the 'God' in him? Although it is undeniable that Walter is often boorish and violent in this often hostile domestic environment, it is also true that we rarely get a glimpse of the appalling work conditions that produce his irritability and exhaustion. So there is bias and imbalance in the authorial commentary on Walter Morel here, as elsewhere in the novel, in favour of Mrs Morel's virtues and philosophy of life, though the actual events as presented by Lawrence give a more balanced picture.

(e) *Search for anything distinctive about the passage, particularly in the area of style, which you have not already noted.* I have nothing further to add here, so I shall move on.

4 *Select a third passage for discussion*

So far I have concentrated on the Morel's family situation and by looking carefully at two passages I feel I know substantially more about it. It is now time to look more closely at Paul and his relationship with his mother, the most important relationship in his life. Here is a passage from the next chapter:

> Presently, Paul was bidden call upon Thomas Jordan, Manufacturer of Surgical Appliances, at 21 Spaniel Row, Nottingham. Mrs Morel was all joy.
>
> 'There you see!' she cried, her eyes shinning. 'You've only written four letters, and the third is answered. You're lucky, my boy, as I've always said you were.'

Paul looked at the picture of a wooden leg, adorned with elastic stockings and other appliances, that figured on Mr Jordan's note-paper, and he felt alarmed. He had not known that elastic stockings existed. And he seemed to feel the business world, with its regulated system of values, and its impersonality, and he dreaded it. It seemed monstrous also that a business could be run on wooden legs.

Mother and son set off together one Tuesday morning. It was August and blazing hot. Paul walked with something screwed up tight inside him. He would have suffered much physical pain rather than this unreasonable suffering at being exposed to strangers, to be accepted or rejected. Yet he chattered away with his mother. He would never have confessed to her how he suffered over these things, and she only partly guessed. She was gay, like a sweetheart. She stood in front of the ticket-office at Bestwood, and Paul watched her take from her purse the money for the tickets. As he saw her hands in their old black kid gloves getting silver out of the worn purse, his heart contracted with pain of love of her.

She was quite excited, and quite gay. He suffered because she *would* talk aloud in the presence of the other travellers. (pp. 113–14)

(a) *Make a statement of what the passage is about.* This passage shows Paul, with the help and support of his mother, setting off with her for his first job interview.

(b) *Search for an opposition or tension within the passage.* As I see it, the tension here is within Paul himself: between his love and regard for his mother and his fear of the outside world. There is a subsidiary tension, derived from this, between his mother's excitement at the outing and his own more dubious feelings.

(c) *Analyse the details of the passage, relating them to the opposition already noted.* In the details of the wooden leg and elastic stockings Lawrence captures very well both the drabness and the bizarre strangeness of the industrial world; in particular its systematised abstraction and specialisation: 'It seemed monstrous also that a business could be run on wooden legs.' This contrasts with the very particular and loving detail of his mother's gloves and worn purse as she searches for the fare money. A whole life of sacrifice and self-denial is summed up in this image. Paul is so responsive to it because he has witnessed that struggle amid adversity; it has helped bond them together. Paul's care for his mother's feelings is shown in the way he hides his apprehensions from her while she, on her part, is all vivacity and enthusiasm, like a young girl. The hot August day seems to confirm her mood while he suffers. Appropriately in a young adolescent, he finds difficulty in exposing a close, private relationship to the gaze of the public world. In her general uncomplicated excitement Mrs Morel seems, if anything, younger than her son.

(d) *Try to say how the passage relates to the novel as a whole.* To me this shows the most positive side of Mrs Morel as she urges her son on. It captures her social ambition for Paul – 'You're lucky, my boy' – but also her unabashed zest for life. Though retrospectively we might feel the relationship is rather too intense – Lawrence does write here of Mrs Morel as 'gay, like a sweetheart' – I think to make this sinister or unwholesome in the light of Paul's subsequent development is to be wise after the event. I find this a touching episode, showing a mother's love at its triumphant best. Such episodes makes Paul's subsequent dependence understandable if no less tragic. It is the first of several trips these two take together, trips that form part of the rhythm of the book. In the next chapter there is the visit to the Leivers family farm, again full of excitement and interest and momentous for Paul; there is a visit to Lincoln in chapter 9 where again we have a lovers' intensity but qualified now by age and disillusionment. Finally, at the end of chapter 13, Mrs Morel's last trip home from Sheffield to die is also made into an adventure, the vitality of spirit resisting the dying body. It is important that we pick up such significant repetitions of events and episodes. They help give the text its distinctive shape.

(e) *Search for anything distinctive in the passage, particularly in the area of style, which you have not already noted.* Again, I have nothing further to say under this heading.

5 *Select a fourth passage for discussion*

The three passages I have looked at have given me some awareness of the complex forces that have shaped Paul's character during his early years. I am more aware than I was of the nature of the struggle between his parents, his animosity towards his father and his debt to his mother. Moreover, I can substantiate my impressions by referring to details I have discovered through close reference to the text.

You could do the same by examining three different passages.

Your conclusion, I expect, would be broadly similar to mine, but your emphasis would be different becausee yyour choice of detail would be different. It would be your reading not mine. Your analysis of the family's relationship would differ from mine to a lesser or greater degree because you are not me – and that's how it should be. The important thing is to back up your insights with the evidence that only a careful close reading will give you.

I think it is time we examined a passage where Paul is shown trying to make a relationship outside the family. Here he is with Miriam on one of his visits to the farm:

> She looked at her roses. They were white, some incurved and holy, others expanded in an ecstasy. The tree was dark as a shadow. She lifted her hand impulsively to the flowers; she went forward and touched them in worship.
>
> 'Let us go,' he said.
>
> There was a cool scent of ivory roses – a white, virgin scent. Something made him feel anxious and imprisoned. The two walked in silence.
>
> 'Till Sunday,' he said quietly, and left her; and she walked home slowly, feeling her soul satisfied with the holiness of the night. He stumbled down the path. And as soon as he was out of the wood, in the free open meadow, where he could breathe, he started to run as fast as he could. It was like a delicious delirium in his veins.
>
> Always when he went with Miriam, and it grew rather late, he knew his mother was fretting and getting angry about him – why, he could not understand. As he went into the house, flinging down his cap, his mother looked up at the clock. She had been sitting thinking, because a chill to her eyes prevented her reading. She could feel Paul being drawn away by this girl. And she did not care for Miriam. (pp. 210–11)

(a) *Make a short statement of what the passage is about.* This passage occurs in the first chapter of Part II. It describes part of an intense experience that Miriam and Paul share, or Miriam attempts to share with Paul, as they look at a wild-rose bush in the twilight. Paul then returns home to his mother.

(b) *Search for an opposition or tension within the passage.* Evidently Paul is caught in an internal conflict of loyalty between Miriam and his mother. Bound into this are a number of ambiguous tensions that express Paul's confusion. The outer world of nature seems associated with Miriam, while the safer and more familiar world of home and domestic routine belongs to Mrs Morel. She seems the spirit of restraint here – quite a shift from the last passage, where she was the driving force for adventure and change. The antithesis is not a simple one, however: Paul feels 'anxious and imprisoned' outside with Miriam, yet he runs home only to enter resentfully and guiltily. He seems to have exchanged one prison for another.

(c) *Analyse the details of the passage, relating them to the opposition already noted.* Miriam is associated with the roses, white, pure and virginal, and both share a religious intensity. The flowers are 'holy' or 'expanded in an ecstasy' and Miriam is moved to worship them. While Miriam is satisfied by the experience, Paul is not. He feels uneasy, 'stumbles' in the wood and feels free only when running in the open meadow. His return home is dominated by guilty feelings. If Miriam is associated with white roses, his mother is associated with the clock, and a known domestic routine that Paul's new needs have begun to challenge. The flinging down of the cap is, in effect, the flinging down of a gauntlet. It demonstrates his frustration.

(d) *Try to say how the passage relates to the novel as a whole.* I noted that the last passage was one of several that involved Paul and his mother in trips or adventures and how this seemed to point to a developing pattern. Similarly this passage is one of many intense exchanges between Paul and Miriam or Paul and his mother that make up the substance of the middle portion of the novel (roughly, chapters 7–11). This concerns Paul's struggles to find a sound basis for an adult relationship with his first sweetheart. As here, many of the exchanges with Miriam involve the natural world. Paul's frustrated inability either to reject Miriam or wholeheartedly to surrender to her are the main substance of this part of the narrative. The exterior world so fully documented in the opening chapters, while not forgotten, certainly recedes; the novel here becomes more internalised, more focused on Paul's inner life. Events in the external world, the normal material of plot and narrative sequence, are only a background for Paul's inner development – or failure to develop.

(e) *Search for anything distinctive about the passage, particularly in the area of style, which you have not already noted.* I think we see more obviously here than in previous passages Lawrence stretching language to suggest mood and complex areas of experience not easily expressed straightforwardly. Lawrence is using symbolic associations between people and nature to extend our understanding of Miriam's personality and its effect on Paul. The roses are *white*, thus capturing both Miriam's passionate intensity and her virginal purity. Some are 'incurved', others 'expanded', suggesting her timidity but also her capacity to respond openly and totally to experience. The scent of the roses becomes one with the enveloping aura of Miriam's personality and her religious mood. This is signalled by the unusual figurative language that makes the scent 'cool', 'white' and 'virginal', attributes that one associates with a living body. Yet the roses are also 'ivory', suggesting a kind of deadness in them and, by implication, in Miriam too maybe. It is as if, although outside, the rose bush has been enveloped by Miriam's religiosity and converted into a shrine. All this rather ambiguous experience is subsumed into the 'something' that makes Paul feel claustrophobic and run for freedom, 'delicious delirium in his veins'; this is another example of Lawence placing complex, abstract ideas in a physical context.

6 *Have I achieved a sufficiently complex sense of the novel?*

I have looked at four passages that deal with Paul's family context and his own developing relationship with his parents and Miriam. But even if I extend and refine what I already know, the answer to this question would still be no. There is still Paul's affair with Clara to consider, and this is important in the last third of the novel. I shall pick a final passage towards the end of the novel in an attempt to rectify this omission.

> And he was to sit all the evening beside her beautiful naked arm, watching the strong throat rise from the strong chest, watching the breasts under the green stuff, the curve of her limbs in the tight dress. Something in him hated her again for submitting him to this torture of nearness. And he loved her as she balanced her head and stared straight in front of her, pouting, wistful, immobile, as if she yielded herself to her fate because it was too strong for her. She could not help herself; she was in the grip of something bigger than herself. A kind of eternal look about her, as if she were a wistful sphinx, made it necessary for him to kiss her. He dropped his programme, and crouched down on the floor to get it, so that he could kiss her hand and wrist. (p. 396)

(a) *Make a short statement of what the passage is about.* This passage is taken from chapter 12, significantly entitled 'Passion', where Paul, finally rejecting Miriam, seeks a physical relationship with Clara. At this point they are already lovers and Paul has taken Clara to the theatre in Nottingham.

(b) *Search for an opposition or tension within the passage.* The most obvious opposition is between physical need and social restraint, a tension both feel; this is emphasised by the theatre in which they sit. A theatre is a public place where people are socially 'on show', yet the lovers are forced to sit in close proximity, which stimulates their desire. This has the effect of producing frustration and a strong inner tension in Paul himself.

(c) *Analyse the details of the passage, relating them to the opposition already noted.* The passage stresses Clara's physical presence and Paul's awareness of it. Her arms, throat, chest, breasts, thighs are all noted, as is the manner in which her body is restrained by her dress. Paul's frustration is expressed in paradox: he both loves and hates her; her proximity is a torture to him. Paul's consciousness is at the centre and we share his conflict of emotion. Clara, on the other hand, is seen more externally as a mysterious object, 'a wistful sphinx'. While she sits immobile, Paul is frenzied both in consciousness and action. He drops the programme to kiss her hand, but Clara is passive: she 'yields' to her fate, swept along by forces outside herself.

(d) *Try to say how the passage relates to the novel as a whole.* The social context of the passage, the Theatre Royal in Nottingham, points to the looser, more impersonal urban world in which Clara is located, a world of work and social roles. Paul courts Clara in snatched hours and half-days from Jordan's, where he is her official superior. Indeed, he is instrumental in getting her the job. Their affair is largely determined by the rhythm of work; its passion, its physical intensity exist despite their social identities and work roles, where much hostility is shown. Thus the tensions and difficulties of their affair are seen as different, cruder and simpler than those that exist between Paul and Miriam. Most of their difficulties, at least initially, are imposed from outside. This lovemaking can be rapturous when free and unconstrained by society. Paul's needs for Miriam are more introverted and complex. The checks and frustrations experienced in this earlier relationship are not externally imposed but come from within.

(e) *Search for anything distinctive about the passage, particularly in the area of style, which you have not already noted.* In the light of what I have said above, it seems to me that Lawrence's style here is less distinctive than in the previous passage, because what he is writing about – male desire – is more general and impersonal, and his treatment of it is more stereotypical. This is in marked contrast to the Miriam passage I have discussed, where Paul's sensibility is more individually challenged and disturbed by Miriam's proximity.

To summarise so far, I think I have made some progress in constructing an overall analysis. Initially, I wanted all my passages to focus on Paul, but this meant ignoring the very fine early chapters. I felt I had to choose a passage that revealed the conflict between Paul's parents; this confirmed what I had already suspected – namely, that the first part of the novel is dominated by Mrs Morel and is family-centred; it is only in the second part that Paul emerges as the dominant consciousness and the method of narration begins to change: it becomes looser and more internal. Family scenes are still important, but they take place in a wider context of Paul's work, his intellectual and artistic concerns, and his emotional conflicts. It is a paradox that, the more varied the scenes become in the novel's second part, the more shadowy the external world becomes.

Of court I recognise that the route I have taken is partial. I need to examine Paul's relationships in greater detail and, moreover, consider them from the women's point of view. Miriam and Clara are interesting characters in their own right who are shown to have their own needs and desires. I am conscious of having said nothing about the end of the novel, some important minor characters, or indeed the whole wider social context in which the Morel family struggles to survive. I am aware that the novel is full of intense lyrical passages involving natural description where Lawrence's language becomes extraordinarily charged and complex. I need to think more about all this; but I am better informed than I was on Paul's development, his progress as a son and lover.

II Aspects of the novel

One of the basic tensions in any novel is the conflict between the individual and the society in which he, or she, has to live. *Sons and Lovers* begins with a historical survey of the mining industry around the village of Bestwood and the changes that new mining technology brings. In particular Lawrence focuses on housing and the manner in which the disreputable hovels of Hell Row are swept away and replaced by the Bottoms. The Bottoms appear substantial and decent from outside but the reality is rather different.

> The dwelling-room, the kitchen, was at the back of the house, facing inward between the blocks, looking at a scrubby back garden, and then at the ash-pits. And between the rows, between the long lines of ash-pits, went the alley, where the children played and the women gossiped and the men smoked. So, the actual conditions of living in the Bottoms, that was so well built and that looked so nice, were quite unsavoury because people must live in the kitchen, and the kitchens opened on to that nasty alley of ash-pits. (p. 36)

Using the method to analyse this passage that we have followed in previous extracts, we can see that the tension here is between the well-built appearance of the Bottoms and the grim living experiences of those that live there. The actual position of the dwelling-rooms and kitchens looking inwards onto the scrubby back gardens, the alleys and the ash-pits, determine the environment where human expression, the gossiping, playing and smoking, take place. We are thus given the sense in the passage of a social organisation where superficially things look decent and civilised while the reality is actually cramping and unwholesome. Such an opposition between the industrial system in which all have to live and work, on the one hand, and each individual's hopes and energies, on the other, is central to *Sons and Lovers* and an important aspect of the novel. The first half is concerned with Bestwood, with the struggles of Gertrude and Walter placed in the wider industrial context in which we learn to see Walter as a typical miner and Gertrude as the exceptional miner's wife. As she says to herself while waiting for the return of her husband from the works in chapter 1, 'I wait, and what I wait for can never come' (p. 41). She yearns for change in Morel, change that runs against the facts of his working life.

Bestwood is a mining community, and the industrial system and its values determine every aspect of its inhabitants' lives. The first part of the novel is rich with sociological details that demonstrate this fact. We can see that, though the hostility of Paul's mother and father may be extreme, the division of labour within the mining community encourages antagonism between men and women generally. Men are enslaved to the demands of the pit. They return exhausted and eager for undemanding relaxation in the pub. Their wives must scrimp and save, eke out and make do, keeping a jealous eye on their housekeeping money. Against the little triumphs of the Morel household, a prize won, a bargain made, lies the sense of the powerlessness of individuals in the grip of an impersonal system. Walter is victimised for his insubordination, family finance is subject to the vicissitudes of the market, relations between employers and employed are remote and hostile. Paul, for example, is bossed and humiliated in chapter 4 when he collects his father's money at the company office.

Lawrence, however, also shows us the community's positive side too. Though Mrs Morel sees herself as superior to those around her, when times are hard she is well supported by those common bonds that reveal themselves in shared adversity. The other women rally round at Paul's birth and there is club money when Walter is sick or injured. If the rough warmth of the pub heals Walter's hurt pride, his wife has the visits of the clergyman and her Monday evenings at the Woman's Guild. Above all there is the intense loyalty and love within the family, which are clearly demonstrated in times of joy and pain. Think of William's first Christmas home from London at the end of chapter 4.

This full and careful treatment of community that is such a feature of the first part of *Sons and Lovers* is an important aspect of the novel. But novels are more than records of sociological information; novels must grow and develop. As I have said, fictions are built on tension and conflict. I am now at a stage to see that *Sons and Lovers* is very much concerned with the struggle of individuals to free themselves from bonds that are both supportive and limiting. Lawrence's careful illustration of community life provides the background for the biographies of several rather extraordinary individuals, characters who have in some way become at odds with their roots, their origins, and who consequently experience stress, suffering and dissatisfaction.

Paul is, of course, pre-eminent in this respect, and we have already gained a sense of this from our basic analysis; but there are others, and, in order to fill out my sense of the novel's theme, I have chosen to dwell briefly on Paul's brother William, and Paul's two lovers, Miriam and Clara. When you feel that you have got hold of a central theme in a fiction such as this, it is worth reading around and seeing if you can find further examples and variations. It is a way of giving the text organisation and pattern.

Mrs Morel initially pours all her energy into giving William expectations and ambition. As the heading of chapter 3 suggests, she 'takes him on'. She refuses to allow him down the pit and sets him on the road that leads from the local co-op to a responsible job in London. Material advancement leads to social advancement. William mixes with his betters and becomes engaged to a girl with social pretensions. He is, in fact, fulfilling his mother's dream when she dressed him up as a middle-class baby. What Lawrence goes on to reveal is the cruel paradox behind Mrs Morel's ambition. On one hand she wishes her sons to find status and fulfilment in the wider world, yet on the other she still wishes them to live for her and not grow away. This, of course, is nonsense, but it causes both mother and sons great pain.

William's gradual disillusionment with Gyp, who is indispensable for 'some things' (p. 176), as he tells his mother, but is no substitute for the family ties he has loosened, begins to tell. His death itself is a great family tragedy and brings out some wonderfully moving writing from Lawrence: you might examine Mrs Morel's visit to London, Morel's reception of the news at the pit-head and the arrival of the coffin at the house, all at the end of chapter 6. But William's brief life, his early promise blighted, has a wider significance: it emphasises the danger, pain and cost of upward mobility and social emancipation. The difficulty of living unsupported by a close community and reinforced by society seems a major preoccupation of Lawrence's and one we can lose sight of if we choose to concentrate on Paul's emotional difficulties to the exclusion of other things.

If William's life is a prefiguration of Paul's, an anticipatory illustration of the dangers as well as the triumphs of ambitious mother-love, Miriam and Clara serve as interesting parallels to each other. It is true that our first impression is one of contrast: Miriam is dark, intense and spiritual; Clara is blond, languid and physical. They offer Paul alternative kinds of love; they minister to differing needs that he seems incapable of reconciling in a single relationship. Again, if we choose to focus on Paul, they become subordinate to him and his problems. As this is the way we are invited to read the book, you may feel this is fair enough. It is appropriate that we view Paul's lovers from his point of view and his needs. From such a reading we get a sense of Paul's psychological dilemma, caught as he is between his desire for mental stimulation and physical fulfilment.

The problem of such a reading is that it is reductive. The text is richer, the portrayal of Miriam and Clara fuller and more ambiguous than this suggests. Undoubtedly the stereotypes I have suggested are there in the portrayal of these two women – that is, in the way Paul and Lawrence choose to see them – but that is no reason why we should see them in the same way. Lawrence, the social observer, is sometimes at variance with Lawrence the psychological analyst, and the book is richer, the characters more complex, because of this. That Miriam is an interesting character in her own right can perhaps best be seen by looking at this passage that features her in her family surroundings:

> Miriam was moving about preparing dinner. Paul watched everything that happened. His face was pale and thin, but his eyes were quick and bright with life as ever. He watched the strange, almost rhapsodic way in which the girl moved about, carrying a great stew-jar to the oven, or looking in the saucepan. The atmosphere was different from that of his own home where everything seemed so ordinary. When Mr Leivers called loudly outside to the horse, that was reaching over to feed on the rose-bushes in the garden, the girl started, looked round with dark eyes, as if something had come breaking in on her world. There was a sense of silence inside this house and out. Miriam seemed as in some dreamy tale, a maiden in bondage, her spirit dreaming in a land far away and magical. And her discoloured, old blue frock and her broken boots seemed only like the romantic rags of King Cophetua's beggar-maid. (p. 194)

Family life at Willey Farm is seen as very different from the Morels' at Bestwood because of the religious intensity that Mrs Leivers brings to her domestic duties. Miriam shares her mother's intensity, as is shown here by the way she moves about her business, but, unlike her mother, she cannot reconcile herself to the role of domestic menial. King Cophetua fell in love with a beggar maid and rescued her from her humble condition.

The young Miriam yearns for a similar rescue. Though we see her through Paul's eyes here, his perception of her romantic idealism and discontent only reinforces notions we know she has of herself as a swine-girl princess or Walter Scott heroine. Her father's shout that breaks her reveries emphasises that she is in a farming environment but not of it. It is a male world of drudgery and exploitation that seeks to scorn if not crush her finer spirit. Despite the charm, the natural beauty around the farm that Paul responds so warmly to, for Miriam this environment offers no such simple release. For her it is a working environment as Bestwood's collieries are for Paul's family. Like Paul, she needs to break free; unlike Paul, she has no male advantages. Mrs Morel sees to it that her son learns some French, German and mathematics from his godfather, the local clergyman, but Miriam must learn her French and algebra through Paul and his good offices of friendship. As education is the only way she can achieve emancipation, Miriam's confusion in attempting to reconcile earnest, disinterested pursuit of knowledge with the emotional draw of friendship is very understandable. It is too easy to condemn Miriam, in Paul's terms, as spiritually rapacious and not to see that her intensity is at least partly determined by the social situation that they both share but that gives her lover unfair advantages. They are kindred spirits, but it is a comradeship that Paul refuses to acknowledge, seeking instead to make her a commonplace sexual mate.

I do not think you will find *Sons and Lovers* an easy novel when it comes to apportioning blame for failed relationships, whether it be that of Paul's parents or his own. In this respect, as in others, Lawrence's open and indeterminate art is remarkably faithful to our experience of life as we lead it. What I do feel, however, is that Miriam's desolation and pain at the end of the novel is every bit as real as Paul's, and both reflect the difficulties of breaking free from limiting circumstances.

Now let us take a look at Clara in her surroundings. I have chosen a passage where Paul sees her at work in her mother's home in Nottingham.

> She spun steadily at her work. He experienced a thrill of joy, thinking she might need his help. She seemed denied and deprived of so much. And her arm moved mechanically, that should never have been subdued to a mechanism, and her head was bowed to the lace, that never should have been bowed. She seemed to be stranded there among the refuse that life has thrown away, doing her jennying. It

> was a bitter thing to her to be put aside by life, as if it had no use for her. No wonder she protested. (p. 321)

It seems to me that this takes up again the opposition I have noted in earlier passages – namely, of individuality and life energy being cramped or stifled by the forces of society. Like Paul and Miriam, Clara is a prisoner, but in this case of wider industrial circumstances, for she has poor job opportunities and the social stigma of marital breakdown. She is a woman alone. Unlike Paul and Miriam, her restrictions are entirely material, her fine arms and head bowed to the act of jennying the lace. I get a sense that Paul and Miriam's damaging inhibitions are as much a product of their minds – the effect of strong mothers and family upbringing, which are a more interior form of social conditioning – while Clara's difficulties are clear for all to see. She has been 'stranded', 'thrown away' by society. It also occurs to me that this passage takes up and confirms an idea that I was mulling over when dealing with the Miriam passage – namely, that Clara, like Miriam, is literally at Paul's mercy. He feels a 'thrill of joy, thinking that she might need his help'. This is not to suggest that Paul is a strong character, simply to suggest that as a man he has certain advantages invested in the system as a whole.

You might look at other passages where Paul woos Clara at Jordans later. I think you will find that they confirm this view. Despite our sense that Paul is really rather a weak character, both women end up as victims, not because Paul is vindictive but because the social system supports his weakness and breaks or subdues their strength. You may feel that the way Lawrence writes the book does this too.

For example, we are encouraged by Paul, and indeed by the way Lawrence writes about her, to view Clara as Miriam's opposite, flesh to her spirit. We can see this in the theatre passage I quoted earlier and I am sure you can find plenty of others that emphasise her physical presence and its magnetic attraction for Paul. Yet, as we have noted, she does share with Miriam a common sense of frustration, and Lawrence makes her potentially even more complex. She has extraordinary aspirations and strength of purpose, as is indicated by her refusal to accept a poor marriage, her political consciousness as a suffragette, and her interest in book learning, yet Paul chooses to ignore these complexities and complications in her character; as his perspective dominates the book, Lawrence does not choose to expand and develop them either. Instead she becomes more and more passive until Paul hands her back to her husband. You may feel that this rather defeated conclusion to her story does not really accord with other details about her that we have learnt earlier.

Similarly as readers we may feel rather coerced into accepting Paul's, and his mother's, judgement of Miriam at face value, though there is plenty of evidence that Lawrence provides as overall narrator that complicates this picture. Miriam is often attacked for being too oppressively spiritual, and episodes such as the hen picking grain from her hand in chapter 6 and Paul giving her a swing in chapter 7 seem to point to an excessive physical timidity that supports this view. Yet Paul's insistent criticism that she is some kind of spiritual vampire and even, finally, a nun is consistently contradicted by the actual descriptions we have of her.

Here is a typical example from the long and complex scene in chapter 8, 'Strife in Love', when Paul burns the bread:

> 'Look,' he said quietly, 'the past participle conjugated with *avoir* agrees with the direct object when it precedes.'
>
> She bent forward, trying to see and to understand. Her free, fine curls tickled his face. He started as if they had been red hot, shuddering. He saw her peering forward at the page, her red lips parted piteously, the black hair springing in fine strands across her tawny, ruddy cheek. She was coloured like a pomegranate for richness. His breath came short as he watched her. Suddenly she looked up at him. Her dark eyes were naked with their love, afraid, and yearning. (p. 262)

All the evidence here points to Paul's abstractness, constraint and inhibition. Miriam's physical presence is fully realised in a warm, sensuous, even exuberant manner. Her hair is free and unrestrained, her lips open, and her complexion glows with healthy vitality. Although apprehensive, she 'yearns' for Paul openly while he retracts in fear.

What are we to conclude from this? Well, it seems to me that another important aspect of *Sons and Lovers* is its autobiographical nature and the consequences this has on the way it is written. Some, though certainly not all, of the material is very close to Lawrence's own early life and upbringing. It is not necessary to know this, but I think it confirms what I have already shown in Lawrence's treatment of both Paul's lovers and his parents – namely, a certain inconsistency, openness and even unreliability in the apparent contradiction between the narrator's commentary or presentation and the facts. On the one hand Lawrence desperately wants to make sense of Paul's struggles; on the other he also wishes to write a full history of provincial Midland life during the last quarter of the nineteenth century. We are back again to the tension between the individual and society. The novelist needs both to write a successful fiction, but the way in which Lawrence treats both is not consistent: it reveals a tension in himself. To make Paul a hero entails a certain bias or suppression of other social facts that Lawrence feels bound to include. Thus, as we have seen, it is possible to create a much more sympathetic portrait of Paul's father or his two lovers from evidence in the text which the text itself, shaped to Paul's needs and point of view, seeks to suppress.

When you read criticism of *Sons and Lovers* you will find much complicated and contradictory discussion of this problem of Lawrence's fairness towards his characters. Some critics will show there is a distinct bias towards Paul and his mother. They will suggest that Lawrence is seeking to explain and justify his own development through Paul's. Others, with equal truth, will show Lawrence's remarkable perception of Paul's weakness in his inability to love any woman wholly while his mother lives. They will show how Walter Morel is created with sympathy and compassion despite the damaging authorial commentary. How can we reconcile these apparently irreconcilable positions? Some critics see such ambiguity as a source of confusing weakness, but I am more inclined to see such contradictions as an enriching strength: any substantial literary text will offer a variety of meanings. There is no simple answer and it is up to all of us to make up our own minds by close, attentive reading. Whatever your conclusions, and they may be very different from mine, do make sure you draw them from the text itself rather than exterior commentary. That way your essays will be less muddled and carry far more weight and conviction.

So far in this section I have concentrated on the social aspects of *Sons and Lovers*, the way in which Lawrence shows his characters interacting with society and being shaped by it. I should now like to move on to another, apparently quite different aspect of the novel: Lawrence's treatment of the natural world. You do not have to read very far in *Sons and Lovers* to sense that Lawrence is using natural description in a particularly intense and dramatic way. Here is a passage from the episode that concludes chapter 4 where Walter locks Gertrude outside in the garden:

> She hurried out of the side garden to the front, where she could stand as if in an immense gulf of white light, the moon streaming high in front of her, the moonlight standing up from the hills in front, and filling the valley where the Bottoms crouched, almost blindingly. There panting and half weeping in reaction from the stress, she murmured to herself over and over again: 'The nuisance! the nuisance!'
>
> She became aware of something about her. With an effort she roused herself to see what it was that penetrated her consciousness. The tall white lilies were reeling in the moonlight, and the air was charged with their perfume as with a presence. Mrs Morel gasped slightly in fear. She touched the big, pallid flowers on their petals, then shivered. They seemed to be stretching in the moonlight. She put her hand into one white bin: the gold scarcely showed on her fingers by moonlight.
>
> She bent down to look at the binful of yellow pollen; but it only appeared dusky. Then she drank a deep draught of the scent. It almost made her dizzy. (pp. 59–60)

The sense I get here is of the awesome power of nature expressed by the brightness and extensiveness of the moonlight, but also by its strangeness, its 'otherness' and apartness from people and human works as this is experienced by Mrs Morel in her reaction to the lilies. Nature is extraordinarily purposeful. The moonlight 'stands up' from the hills and fills the valleys. Under its influence the lilies 'reel', 'stretch' and 'charge' the air with their perfume, while buildings 'crouch' submissively. Mrs Morel is vulnerable here, cast out from her familiar domestic setting. In its daytime aspect nature can be used to console, to provide a recreational release. There are many examples of Mrs Morel rejoicing in flowers, seeking in their artless fulfilment a consolation for a life thwarted and unfulfilled. But here, at night, the tables are turned; nature interrogates her. The presence of the lilies is menacing: full of pollen and 'reeling' with the intoxication of their own scent, they seem to be associated with the male fertilising power of Walter, the drunken husband she wishes to reject but whose child she is carrying. Well may she murmur repeatedly, 'The nuisance! The nuisance!' or 'gasp with fear', for she too is caught up in the process of nature that she may rebel against but is powerless to resist. Although she seeks to reassert her intellectual curiosity and hence her human individuality by examining the pollen, the moonlight renders such examination useless; instead the scent makes her dizzy and rather powerless.

If you read on, the episode concludes with Mrs Morel going to bed: 'As she unfastened her brooch at the mirror, she smiled faintly to see her face all smeared with the yellow dust of lilies' (p. 62). How are we to interpret this 'faint smile'? Are we to gather that she has had to acknowledge the power of forces stronger than she – perhaps even acknowledge them in herself – through this humbling experience, or is it a derisory ironic smile as, safe inside, she seeks to confirm her own conscious individuality before brushing the evidence of her humiliation away? The text gives us no clues, providing another example of Lawrence's openness of method.

Such passages show Lawrence using the natural world to open up or suggest whole areas of his characters' personalities that are not susceptible to analysis in the usual social ways. They reveal Lawrence developing a new and innovatory method. By placing his characters, often at moments of crisis, in nature rather than apart from it, Lawrence redefines and extends our normal sense of what we mean by 'character'. He seeks to express our instinctive drives, our inarticulate inner psychic being on which we all have to build social identities. In a crude kind of way I could say that Lawrence is interested in the 'animal' in us, that set of basic impulses towards survival, health and fulfilment that all natural things share and that brings us into much closer relationship with the natural world than is usual in novels, where people are invariably set against nature as something to be mastered.

But, if Lawrence sees human beings as animals, it is as very complex animals capable of building complex institutions and societies. However, if these institutions and modes of human organisation take us too far away from the 'animal' in us – that is, our own instinctive inner life – then pain and suffering will be the result, for in Lawrence's fiction the natural world is dynamic, vital, alive, and his characters can only find themselves fully when in intuitive accord with it. This makes Lawrence into a very special kind of social novelist whose criticisms of industrial society are more radical and far-reaching than those of authors who limit themselves to attacking poverty and exploitation in a material sense alone.

These insights require new methods and new priorities and I think we can see Lawrence beginning to develop these, especially in the second half of *Sons and Lovers*. I expect you found, as I did, that the early chapters give you few difficulties. Mr and Mrs Morel are presented fully and their conflict is clearly explained; it was the consequence of social and cultural differences that initially drew them together but finally tore them apart. The family kitchen is the centre of the first part, but the relationship between the Morels' private domestic struggle and the wider social reality of a mining community is richly documented.

While the opening chapters are written with unusual flair, there is nothing very new in them, though passages such as the moon episode I have just discussed might alert you to Lawrence's more distinctive gifts. It is when we move on to Paul's problems and his mother's love ceases to be a simple good that we realise that the novel is not evolving in any expected and obvious manner. If the major theme of *Sons and Lovers* is the education of Paul Morel, it is an education that does not proceed in any very straightforward way. Most novelists would treat Paul's struggles to climb the social ladder and his conflict with the external world of ambition, promotion and success. This is present here but only in a faint and outlined way. It is not Lawrence's prime concern. The central issue is Paul's failed relationships, and there is a lack of plot in any conventional sense. Instead we get a series of intimate scenes where Paul is forced to confront and finally learn to acknowledge his inadequacies as a lover. The shape and organisation of the novel seem to express this sense of failure. Instead of a confident, forward-moving narrative, we get a whole series of cycles and repetitions as Paul is torn between his conflicting needs and loyalties. Again and again he resolves to free himself from Miriam, only to return, and, when he enters a new relationship with Clara, this provides only temporary relief. He seems doomed to repeat the self-defeating struggles of his parents within himself; his inability to reconcile his spiritual and bodily needs recapitulates in a more interior, psychological way their marital incompatibility. A whole legacy of guilt and failure is carried forward into Paul's life and this unifies the two parts of the novel. The carefully documented first half sets up the conditions by which we can understand Paul's plight in the second.

Finally, I should like to discuss another aspect of the novel's form – namely, Lawrence's use of a symbolic method to draw together apparently unrelated scenes and thus give the book coherence and pattern. I have mentioned Lawrence's need to evolve new methods in order to express new insights, and the novel's lack of plot in any orthodox sense. Instead of any clear logical pattern of cause and effect, we follow Paul through a number of intimate encounters involving discussion and self-examination. Can we link these together to give the novel a meaningful shape as distinct from the loose, episodic sequence of events in a young man's early life?

I think we can once we understand the organic relationships that exist in Lawrence's fictional world, where everything is related to everything else. For example, Paul's inner distress, his struggle between his urge for life and his desire for death, does not exist in a vacuum: it is part of a wider struggle that is enacted throughout society as a whole. Everywhere in *Sons and Lovers*, forces and instincts that lead towards life and fulfilment are being perverted or blocked and so redirected towards frustration and death. Lawrence underlines the connection by the repeated use of images of sickness and disease that act as a powerful co-ordinating device, more in the manner of a poem than a novel. Such repeated use of related images and scenes give the book a tighter organisation than it appears to have when we are first reading it for the story.

So William's mysterious illness, Baxter Dawes's typhoid, Walter Morel's degeneration and Mrs Morel's cancer are used in a figurative as well as a literal way to expose not just the stress within Lawrence's characters but the sickness within society generally. It is as if the unnatural and destructive relationship of Paul's parents spreads outwards, permeating the book as a whole. Lawrence wrote to his friend Edward Garnett concerning *Sons and Lovers*, 'One sheds one's sicknesses in books – repeats and presents again one's emotions to be master of them.' This is what Paul too attempts to do. He is sick but his sickness is not of his own making. He struggles to make himself whole. Everything he does in the last stages of the novel is an attempt to heal himself.

I expect you found Paul's friendship with Baxter Dawes rather odd, and his treatment of Clara at the end by handing her back to her husband inexplicable. These actions make better sense if you see them as part of Paul's gathering awareness of the tragic impasse in which he finds himself, and his growing reassessment of his parents. Part of him wishes to die, to give up, but the will to live is strong as in any animal. He sees in Baxter Dawes a fellow sufferer, a cruder version of his own despair, someone he needs to forgive as he singularly fails to forgive his own father, whom Baxter strikingly resembles. The giving-back of Clara is symbolic restitution also; it is an attempt to heal the rift between man and wife, to reconstitute in different terms his parents' failed relationship. It is indicative of his growing understanding of his situation. Similarly, the giving-back of Clara is linked to his mother's illness. He sees the necessity to destroy the mother and release her substitutes, Miriam and Clara, before he can go free.

Mrs Morel's death is deeply distressing and is the point where the public, social and the private, psychological elements in the tale are most intimately fused. It shows how far Lawrence, a twentieth-century novelist, has moved away from traditional morality and the consolations of orthodox religion. It is a terminal image that reveals a whole system of society discredited and run-down. Somehow, out of this wreckage, Paul must build a new life, if he can. Like the rest of the novel, the end is open and unresolved. If *Sons and Lovers* is an 'education' novel, it is in a new and tragic way. We cannot be sure that Paul has mastered his situation or is capable of acting on his knowledge.

I talked at the beginning of this section of the conflict between the individual and society as essential to any fiction. What I hope to have shown is how, in his first major novel, Lawrence has already begun to reinterpret this relationship in a particularly distinctive way that is to have important consequences for the organisation of his later novels.

4

The Rainbow (1915)

I Constructing an overall analysis

The Rainbow is a most unusual novel and I doubt that you have read anything quite like it before. Certainly a reading of *Sons and Lovers* will not have prepared you for Lawrence's sudden and dramatic change of method. The important thing is not to panic at this stage and go consulting criticism that might confuse you or prejudice your own responses. Keep to a method that forces you to confront the text on your terms, and helps you organise your own thoughts and impressions. By doing this you will 'possess' the text more securely for yourself: you will think more clearly and, ultimately, write much better. I am going to follow the same procedures as before to construct my initial analysis, so

1 *After reading the novel, think about the story and what kind of pattern you can see in the text*

This is my version of events:

> The subject of *The Rainbow* is the early life-histories of three generations of a Midland family called the Brangwens. The novel opens in the 1840s with an account of some industrial changes in the Erewash valley, where they live, and ends just after the Boer War at the turn of the twentieth century. Initially the novel concentrates on Tom Brangwen, an affluent young farmer who, feeling a sense of dissatisfaction in his life, woos and marries an émigré Polish widow, Lydia Lensky. There is an account of their early married life at Marsh Farm and the evolving relationship Tom has with his stepdaughter Anna. The emphasis of the narrative now shifts to Anna. We learn of her growth to maturity, her courtship and marriage

to her cousin Will Brangwen, a lace-designer. There is a long account of the difficulties they experience in their first year of marriage, a bitter conflict of incompatible needs that is only partially resolved at some cost to Will in particular. Once Anna wins this battle their marriage becomes very inward looking and self-sufficient. They have a large family in their small, rural cottage in the village of Cossethay near the family farm. Eventually they move to the nearby town of Beldover when Will becomes an art-and-craft teacher.

Once again the narrative shifts focus, this time to Ursula, their eldest child. Again the emphasis is on her childhood and adolescence, and on her relationship with her father, which proves to be painful and difficult. One episode during her childhood that receives memorable coverage is the death of her grandfather, Tom Brangwen, by drowning when the canal embankment near the farm bursts during a freak storm. The novel goes on to tell of her vague, unsatisfied religious yearnings that a flirtation with Anton Skrebensky, son of one of her grandmother's Polish friends, fails to satisfy. He is an army officer and goes off to the Boer War while Ursula pursues her intense relationship with Winifred Inger, her young, independent class-mistress. This relationship similarly ends in disillusionment, and Ursula is instrumental in marrying Winifred off to her uncle Tom, a colliery manager in the new industrial Yorkshire town of Wiggiston. Ursula leaves school, and the final part of the novel is concerned with her struggle to find a place and some measure of satisfaction in the wider world, independent of her family. To this end she becomes a pupil teacher at a local school in nearby Ilkeston, and, having survived two difficult years there, moves on to University College, Nottingham, to study for a degree. During her final year Skrebensky returns on leave and Ursula sacrifices her degree to have an affair with him. Though Anton expects marriage, Ursula becomes yet again disillusioned with him and the social values he stands for. She rejects him and he goes to India without her. Ursula discovers she is pregnant, miscarries and falls ill. She emerges from this crisis with a stronger sense of her capacities, and the novel ends with her vision of the rainbow, the vision of new hope for all the exploited inhabitants of the new industrial world.

*

Now, you may be baffled as to the significance and meaning of many of the episodes in this novel when you first read it and this is understandable. It is a difficult book and Lawrence's intentions are not at all clear. In their interpretations many critics flatly contradict each other, so that is all the more reason for you to sort out for yourself some basic ideas about the kind of novel it is.

What, then, are my initial impressions of *The Rainbow* based on my synopsis of its events? Well, that it is a 'saga' novel, having a much broader narrative sweep than its predecessor, *Sons and Lovers*, and a different conception of characterisation. I may not be very clear what this new mode of characterisation is, but I know that Will Brangwen, say, is created in a quite different way from Walter Morel, and I need to understand how and why. I have said that *The Rainbow* is a 'saga' novel. By this I mean that there is something heroic – 'larger than life' – in the presentation of the main characters and that they are less shaped and determined by their social roles in the way we have come to expect in most novels. As I look over my synopsis I can see that Lawrence's interest is focused on the way each generation of the Brangwens encounters the great central experiences of life: birth, growing-up, courtship, marriage and death. These experiences are open and common to all humanity, yet each generation seems to experience them rather differently. So, looking for my basic pattern, I can see in these life-histories a demonstration of continuity and change, repetition yet also variety. Instead of plot as we normally think of it, a sequence of events that follows the logic of cause and effect, the narrative movement of *The Rainbow* is more rhythmic and wave-like. Each generation comes to fruition and then falls back, giving way to the next. Thinking about the shape of the novel a little more, I can see the second half of the narrative, 'Ursula's story', has a rather more familiar shape than the first. Though it is a part of the wave-like rhythm I have described, it is also more open and fragmented – like a biograpy. In a sense it is Ursula's education novel; she undergoes a number of varied experiences in a looser, more public social world. Her life is much more obviously shaped by society, a society she is in conflict with, while the lives of the first two generations of Brangwen are more private, more poetically expressed and more enclosed, away from society, around the grand, central experiences I have noted.

Finally, it is worth giving some time to a consideration of the novel's title. Titles often give us clues to the novelist's intention.

The title of this is not 'The Brangwens' but *The Rainbow*: what does this suggest? To me it suggests that Lawrence's central preoccupation is external to the Brangwens themselves; the theme of *The Rainbow* lies beyond the Brangwens, though they provide its essential illustration. If I go on to think about rainbows generally, two notions, one from folklore and one from religious myth, come to mind. First, rainbows are associated with rewards, invariably tantalising or illusory, that are sought after by long journeying. Secondly, and more specifically, the rainbow is God's sign of a covenant, or binding promise, between him and all living things after the Flood (Genesis 9). I may not be too sure as to the relevance of these notions, but they seem worth bearing in mind as I move forward to my next task – namely, to start exploring the text itself in more detail. As before, I am going to start picking and analysing passages in an attempt to construct some sort of overall view of *The Rainbow*; I shall avoid breaking down each step into subsections, but I shall still keep to the same sequence of analysis used in previous chapters.

2 *Select a short passage featuring one of the main characters and try to build upon the ideas you have established so far*

This sets me a problem straightaway. The obvious approach would be to look at Tom, the first important Brangwen, at once. Yet the novel does not encourage us to do this until we have placed him in the context of certain common traits of the Brangwens as a 'race'. This is an odd way of putting it, but then the opening pages of the novel are extremely odd, most unlike the usual novel where characters are placed in a social context. This begins to happen at the opening of the second section, where history announces itself: 'About 1840, a canal was constructed across the meadows of the Marsh Farm . . . ' (p. 46). (Page references to the novel relate to the Penguin edition, 1981). In the introductory section we are asked to look at the Brangwens in a more general, unspecified way; as I feel this must be important for what comes later, I am going to examine two paragraphs that make a distinction between the Brangwen men and the Brangwen women.

> It was enough for the men, that the earth heaved and opened its furrows to them, that the wind blew to dry the wet wheat,

> and set the young ears of corn wheeling freshly round about; it was enough that they helped the cow in labour, or ferreted the rats from under the barn, or broke the back of a rabbit with a sharp knock of the hand. So much warmth and generating and pain and death did they know in their blood, earth and sky and beast and green plant, so much exchange and interchange they had with these, that they lived full and surcharged, their senses full fed, their faces always turned to the heat of the blood, staring into the sun, dazed with looking towards the source of generation, unable to turn round.
>
> But the woman wanted another form of life than this, something that was not blood-intimacy. Her house faced out from the farm-buildings and fields, looked out to the road and the village with church and Hall and the world beyond. She stood to see the far-off world of cities and governments and the active scope of men, the magic land to her, where secrets were made known and desires fulfilled. She faced outwards to where men moved dominant and creative, having turned their back on the pulsing heat of creation, and with this behind them, were set out to discover what was beyond, to enlarge their own scope and range and freedom; whereas the Brangwen men faced inwards to the teeming life of creation, which poured unresolved into their veins. (pp. 42–3)

We can say at once that this is not 'realistic' writing; there is a stress here on major generic differences between the sexes, and these do not bear much relation to common reality. Experience tells us it is impossible for men and women to be so sharply differentiated in their attitudes to life. What we have here is a dramatisation of two extreme positions that have been hooked fairly arbitrarily onto gender differences.

What are these two positions or attitudes towards life? Well, in the attitude of the Brangwen men, Lawrence is showing us an unadventurous involvement in and reliance on the rhythms and cycles of the natural world. For farmers this is natural enough, but Lawrence stresses it to the exclusion of everything else. He calls it 'blood-intimacy'. The Brangwen women, on the other hand, look to the world beyond the farm, to the institutions of civilisation and the realms of mental discovery.

Lawrence stresses the active participation of man in nature: the earth 'heaves' and opens its furrows in a co-operative sexual way to the annual planting. He also stresses nature's self-regulating powers; the wind dries the wet young wheat. If nature is warm and secure, it is also cruel and destructive; the Brangwen men collaborate in both these aspects. They also share in nature's rather inert self-sufficiency, being 'full fed' but dazed and inward-looking.

As for the women, their houses (an odd symbolic detail this) face away from the farms towards the outside world. By this Lawrence seems to suggest that their expectations and mental horizons are quite different from those of their menfolk. Although they cannot move themselves, they yearn to transcend the rooted existence of the farm; they sense the excitement of a progressive civilisation where human possibilities are being shaped, articulated and extended, and they wish to join it.

Thinking about the novel as a whole, this passage seems a good illustration of what I'm going to call its 'quest' theme. Right from the opening pages Lawrence expresses two conflicting impulses in human beings: the need to stand still and the need to move on. He is announcing this here in a rather artificial, poetically heightened way to draw out attention to a fundamental tension that is likely to affect his view of character in this novel generally. The mental pushing-forward of the Brangwen women and the sensual pulling-back of the Brangwen men alerts us to a conflict between mind and body, a kind of rhythmic tug-of-war within human beings as they seek for fulfilment in their lives, that interests Lawrence far more than matters of social ambition. As if to emphasise this conflict, character here is expressed in a simple, heroic way. There are no names, no individualisation; just a direct, simple focus on fulfilment as a necessary urge satisfied, crudely, in the men but not in the women; for them, it demands a reaching-out beyond the needs of nature, a mental challenge as well as physical satisfaction.

Finally, if we look at the language we can see it is deliberately heightened to draw our attention away from the normal daily reality and events that form the substance of most novels. By careful, measured repetition, both of words and of phrasing ('It was enough . . . it was enough', 'so much warmth . . . so much exchange'), balanced antithesis ('She faced outwards . . . whereas the Brangwen men faced inwards') and deliberate biblical cadences, whether in diction ('beast and green plant') or phrasing and rhythm ('where secrets were made known and desires fulfilled'), Lawrence is insisting on the religious intensity and solemnity of his material. This formal patterning of the language illustrates something that I have noted before: namely, that Lawrence is capable of writing in a highly charged, poetic manner; the language itself is a powerful, shaping force in Lawrence's fiction transcending the traditional categories of plot and character.

I think I have now got as much as I can from this passage. If I can summarise my findings, they are as follows: we see here Lawrence using language in a formal, stylised way to demonstrate the conflicting impulses of inertia and growth within human beings. Because this conflict is so elaborately drawn to our attention at the onset of the novel, it suggests to me that this tension is a crucial one, informing and shaping the novel as a whole.

3 *Select a second passage for discussion*

I want to move on now to a passage that focuses on Tom, the first Brangwen to be individualised and whose emotional life is the subject of the first third of the novel. I have chosen a passage towards the end of chapter 5 where Tom is in church at his stepdaughter's wedding.

> Brangwen was staring away at the burning blue window at the back of the altar, and wondering vaguely, with pain, if he ever should get old, if he ever should feel arrived and established. He was here at Anna's wedding. Well, what right had he to feel responsible, like a father? He was still as unsure and unfixed as when he had married himself. His wife and he! With a pang of anguish he realized what uncertainties they both were. He was a man of forty-five. Forty-five! In five more years fifty. Then sixty – then seventy – then it was finished. My God – and one still was so unestablished.
>
> How did one grow old – how could one become confident? He wished he felt older. Why, what difference was there, as far as he felt matured or completed, between him now and him at his own wedding? He might be getting married over again – he and his wife. He felt himself tiny, a little, upright figure on a plain circled round with an immense, roaring sky: he and his wife, two little upright figures walking across this plain, whilst the heavens shimmered and roared about them. When did one come to an end? In which direction was it finished? There was no end, no finish, only this roaring vast space. Did one never get old, never die? This was the clue. He exulted strangely, with torture. He would go on with his wife, he and she like two children camping in the plains. What was sure but the endless sky? But that was so sure, so boundless.
>
> Still the royal blue colour burned and blazed and sported itself in the web of darkness before him, unwearyingly rich and splendid. How rich and splendid his own life was, red and burning and blazing and sporting itself in the dark meshes of his body: and his wife, how

> she glowed and burned dark within her meshes! Always it was so unfinished and unformed! (pp. 173–4)

Tom Brangwen is here taking stock of his life. He has just given Anna away in marriage to Will Brangwen and soon the novel will shift away from him. In a sense, from Lawrence's point of view, his life is effectively spent; its vital, determining experiences are over. Anna's wedding-day marks the end of one cycle of the novel and the beginning of another. Tom's musings are important for they express the furthest point of his consciousness before his life begins to ebb, to fall back into routine and eventually a premature death. At this solemn time, Tom feels acutely the disparity between his yearnings for fulfilment and completion and his present sense of inadequacy and immaturity. He moves on to consider the frightening limitation and vulnerability of the individual life in the grander perspective, the general process of things. Finally he retreats into the immediate physical security and comfort of his physical love for his wife.

I have talked about the 'quest' theme that I see in the novel. I picked this theme out when I tried to make some sense of Lawrence's narrative after constructing a synopsis; it seemed to me that Lawrence was pre-eminently interested in the way that human beings struggle to make some sense, to achieve some fulfilment in their lives. The first passage I have discussed from Lawrence's elaborate introduction has given me some further thoughts on this, and now, moving on to look at Tom Brangwen, I want to see if I can develop these ideas, or discover some new ones. There are plenty of other passages I could have chosen; I did consider analysing something from Tom's wooing of Lydia, for example. Up to a point it doesn't really matter what you choose provided you work at it and try to fit it into some overall strategy or pattern. The fact that we are all drawn to different passages will ensure that all our readings will be slightly different. It is a question of selection and priority, and every new passage we choose will modify our opinions of the book and make them more complex and more sophisticated. It is easy to get confused, however, especially with an author such as Lawrence; that is why we must keep hold of some basic, quite simple ideas and make sure we see them through. From the first passage I got the sense of inertia and growth, rootedness and restlessness, as the twin, conflicting impulses that Lawrence sees as motivating human behaviour. I want to see if I can find them here and I am not disappointed. Tom yearns to feel 'arrived and established' but despairs at being so. In a paradoxical, anguished way he both wants age and the completion that only death can bring and yet, with his hunger for life, he fears it. He also knows that he will never experience the 'arrival', the 'establishment', that he wants. It is not in the nature of life to allow it: 'Always it was so unfinished and unformed!'

As in the earlier passage there is conflict, this time within Tom himself, between a dissatisfied mental search for the articulation of a mystery – 'When did one come to an end? In which direction was it finished? . . . He exulted strangely, with torture' – and his relapse into the 'rooted' sensual satisfaction at his marriage: he and Lydia 'burn', 'blaze' and 'sport' in the 'dark meshes' of their bodies, all of which suggest the 'dazed' introversion, the 'blood knowledge', of the Brangwen men in the first extract.

There are important differences and similarities between this passage and the first I chose. While the first was lyrical and general, this passage shows much more clearly Lawrence's skills as an imaginative novelist. He convincingly dramatises Tom's bewildered thoughts, so developing his character in traditionally accepted ways. This is particularly true of the first paragraph, where Tom's simple thought-processes seem exactly appropriate to the sort of person he is. Where Lawrence begins to show his own particular gifts is in the second and third paragraphs; here he blends Tom's questioning with a more subtle, metaphoric writing that expresses Tom's thoughts in ways that Tom might feel but could not articulate for himself.

This more figurative writing does have links with the first passage and with other, more general thoughts I have had about the novel. I talked at the beginning of this chapter of *The Rainbow* as a 'saga' novel, because it treated its characters in a heroic manner; I felt their lives were explored in ways that were 'larger than life', grander than in most novels. The writing here confirms this. There is something very primitive, biblical even, in the idea of two nomadic figures walking across a plain dwarfed by a vast 'roaring' sky. It doesn't seem to to bear much resemblance to the everyday lives of an affluent Midland farmer and his wife in the mid-nineteenth century. Of course it doesn't and that's the point. Lawrence elevates his writing at such moments to insist on their intensity to those concerned. They confront their destinies, like the patriarchs of the Old Testament, with a seriousness that can only be described as religious, and so the language and the metaphors are entirely appropriate. In such comments their social existence is seen as superficial and gives way to a grander, more elementary sense of self. Of course, the hazardous epic journey which Tom here imagines his life to be is a physical metaphor for a spiritual search that relates to the quest theme I have noted and to my earlier thoughts on Lawrence's use of *The Rainbow* as the title of his novel. As Tom realises, 'there is no end, no finish' to his search. In pursuing the rainbow there is always journeying but no arrival.

One final point about the language I should like to make is the way that it mimes the tension between movement and inertia that I have noted. The second paragraph stresses vista and space, and is full of questions, but the third emphasises the enclosed sensuality of Tom's marriage with its heavy rhythmic repetitions. Lawrence develops the burning blue colour of the stained-glass window as a metaphor for Tom's sensual satisfaction: it is indeed 'rich and splendid' but also enclosed and limiting. 'Meshes', after all, contain and capture.

4 *Select a third passage for discussion*

> His life was shifting its centre, becoming more superficial. He had failed to become really articulate, failed to find real expression. He had to continue in the old form. But in spirit, he was uncreated.
>
> Anna was absorbed in the child now, she left her husband to take his own way. She was willing now to postpone all adventure into unknown realities. She had the child, her palpable and immediate future was the child. If her soul had found no utterance, her womb had.
>
> The church that neighboured with his house become very intimate and dear to him. He cherished it, he had it entirely in his charge. If he could find no new activity, he would be happy cherishing the old, dear form of worship. He knew this little whitewashed church. In its shadowy atmosphere he sank back into being. He liked to sink himself in its hush as a stone sinks into water
>
> He went across his garden, mounted the wall by the little steps, and entered the hush and peace of the church. As the heavy door clanged to behind him, his feet re-echoed in the aisle, his heart re-echoed with a little passion of tenderness and mystic peace. He was also slightly ashamed, like a man who has failed, who lapses back into his fulfilment. (pp. 248–9)

I have chosen here part of Lawrence's commentary on Anna and Will's development after a year of marriage. Though we are denied direct access to the characters' consciousness, we can see the same tension between their potential for self-development and what they have settled for – the urge to move forward and the desire to retreat – that we have noted in earlier passages.

Anna seems to have more easily accepted a limited fulfilment in terms of motherhood. Her womb 'speaks' for her and because of that she is prepared to relinquish more spiritual claims. In this respect she is like the Brangwen men in the first extract. Like them she feels inward 'to the teeming life of creation'; like them she is caught up in the cycles of procreation and 'unable to turn round'.

Will's case is more complex. He is much more aware of the spiritual dimension but lacks the courage to seek it for himself. Anna has forced him to ground his life in her terms. As the previous chapter heading suggests, she is 'Anna Victrix' – Anna the victor. The spiritual side of Will demands satisfaction but he can only express it through a deliberate retreat into the forms of a religion he knows are empty and discredited. Lawrence stresses this by describing Will's attachment to church ritual in regressive, rather sensual terms that emphasise its superficiality. He 'sinks' back into being like a stone in the water, this rather inert image together with the repetition of 'sink' emphasises Will's defeat, his failure of spiritual expression. He likes the enclosed, undemanding safety of the church and 'the old, dear form of worship' in ways that remind one of his delight in the pleasures of his honeymoon at the beginning of chapter 6. Indeed, in Will sensual and religious needs become more and more difficult to distinguish. He experiences 'a little passion of tenderness' in the church, he 'cherishes' it; it is 'intimate and dear to him'. No wonder he is 'slightly ashamed' and feels he has retreated for his fulfilment. The re-echoing in the church is both physical and emotional and also underlines his defeated self-absorption and retreat from the challenges of life. Lawrence sees Will's case as more painful because he is more aware of lost potential than Anna is.

This is not a particularly difficult passage, though I do feel it gives us some valuable pointers as to how Lawrence wishes us to view Will and Anna's relationship. Comparing it with the other passages we have examined, I am struck by Lawrence's evolving attitude towards orthodox religion as a means of spiritual expression. In the first passage the Brangwen women looked outwards towards the church as a symbol of the 'magic land' where secrets were made known. Indeed, in the opening paragraph of the novel the church tower is a constant reminder to the labouring Brangwens of something standing above and beyond them. For Tom Brangwen the church is a serious place for serious though; his fumbling realisation as to the mystery and brevity of human life find expression in biblical images. By the time we come to examine Anna and Will's struggle I think we are led to see that orthodox religious forms and doctrines are less able to express genuine spiritual needs and aspirations. They are becoming outmoded and, rather than facilitating communication between Will and Anna, become a source of contention and strife. Lawrence uses this as an indication of the gathering complexity of modern life, where relationships can thwart as well as aid fulfilment. Anna here is seen to abandon her husband to find his own way, while Tom saw Lydia and himself going on together 'like two children camping in the plain'. I should need more material to develop the point satisfactorily, but it seems to me that Tom appears very innocent in his simple need for Lydia to give some shape to his life. Will and Anna, by contrast, seem more self-absorbed; they make more complex demands on life and on each other.

5 *Select a fourth passage for discussion*

I could hardly begin to construct a basic analysis of *The Rainbow* without some examination of Ursula, for she dominates the second half of the novel. I have chosen a passage where she is waiting for a tram on her first day at Brinsley Street school.

> As she waited at the tram-terminus she reverted swiftly to her childhood; her teasing grandfather, with his fair beard and blue eyes, and his big, monumental body; he had got drowned: her grandmother, whom Ursula would sometimes say she had loved more than anyone else in the world: the little church school, the Phillips boys; one was a soldier in the Life Guards now, one was a collier. With a passion she clung to the past.
>
> But as she dreamed of it, she heard the tram-car grinding round a bend, rumbling dully, she saw it draw into sight, and hum nearer.

> It sidled round the loop at the terminus, and came to a standstill, looming above her. Some shadowy grey people stepped from the far end, the conductor was walking in the puddles, swinging round the pole.
>
> She mounted into the wet, comfortless tram, whose floor was dark with wet, whose windows were all steamed, and she sat in suspense. It had begun, her new existence. (p. 417)

We can see here a much more obvious opposition between going forward to a new life and retreating to the safe and known, between a comforting past and an uncertain future. The family and her village past give Ursula a sense of identity and continuity, but they are also a tempting regression that she must reject by boarding the tram.

Lawrence heightens the drama in Ursula's situation by making, very naturally, her past memories rather sentimental and idealised. She forgets how niggardly and frustrating she found the constraints of the village school or the companionship of the local children. In contrast, the future is seen as rather threatening and squalid; the tram-car is an ominous introduction to her new life as it grinds round the bend, rumbles dully, sidles towards her and finally looms above her. The general environment with its 'shadowy grey people', wet floor and steamed-up windows does not inspire much confidence. Ursula's journey seems even more fraught with disillusionment and perils than those of the earlier Brangwens.

Lawrence here seems much more open to the external world and the more usual material of novels. Ursula's thoughts and the rather dismal description of the tram terminus are much more directly presented. There is a big difference between the straightforward, almost matter-of-fact mode of narration here and the rhythmical poetic texture of the first extract or the figurative density of the second. This shows that Lawrence can examine the external world and more ordinary experiences in this novel as well as moments of exceptional psychological tension, heightened dramatic seriousness or poetic intensity.

Having said this, if we look carefully at the text, there is a guiding hand and a poetic vision of a sort. After all, it doesn't *have* to be raining on Ursula's first day as a teacher; other people don't *have* to be reduced to pale shadows. The urban scene is deliberately created mean and grubby, a hostile contrast to Ursula's vulnerable aspirations.

As for Ursula herself, we do not get any detailed psychological insight into her character here, but she is earlier recognisably a modern girl taking her decisions in our modern world; we can recognise that it is our modern world because Ursula has to commit herself to the external changes in circumstances and social roles that we all have to make. Her quest involves literal movement, underlined by the tram journey, and this contrasts with the more rooted internal struggles of previous generations. This is evident when we compare Tom Brangwen's metaphysical journey under an 'immense, roaring sky' with the onset of Ursula's career here. The first is splendid and awesome; the second, rather depressing and squalid. By such invidious comparisons Lawrence seems to be implying a criticism of the imaginative poverty of the modern world despite its material advances.

6 *Have I achieved a sufficiently complex sense of the novel?*

So, where have we got so far? On a hint from the title I set out to look for passages with the idea of a quest or search theme in my mind, and with the intention of developing it. Although it was not deliberate, I can see that I have chosen passages showing Tom towards the end of his life quest, Will and Anna in the midst of theirs, and Ursula at the outset of hers. Despite this variety I can see significant similarities that help to co-ordinate the narrative as well as some interesting differences. Above all, I am now confident that an examination of the ways in which people grow and develop – or fail to grow – is a central concern to Lawrence in this novel. To express this he is forced to adapt the form of the novel in quite fundamental ways, because what is central to him is marginal to most novelists and, consequently, most novels. The wave-like structure of the narrative I noted earlier, where different generations of the Brangwen family each encounter similar experiences, is part of this adaptation and a necessary substitution for the more traditional kind of plot. Another adaptation is the denser, more poetic use of language, especially in the earlier passages. This is understandable when we consider that poetry and poetic language is the more usual medium and mode of expression when exploring a sense of self and internal struggles. Indeed, 'growth' in Lawrence's terms involves a struggle between opposites, the known and unknown, flesh and spirit, rest and movement, that the language dramatically enacts: we, the readers, are forced to participate in the struggles of the characters and not merely observe them from outside. From this I sense that Lawrence has a more fluid, open sense of what 'character' is, seeing it more as a place where contending forces struggle for supremacy than as something 'rounded' and complete; but I have yet to explore this in any detail. This is not to say that Lawrence ignores the more traditional skills of creating characters in a social sense or placing them in a social context, but it does suggest that he goes deeper than most novelists, searching out and expressing common experiences and basic needs that underlie surface difference.

If all the characters in these passages reveal a common yearning to reach some final completion of themselves, they differ in the degree to which they are able to achieve it. I suspect that there might be some sort of social criticism at work here, in that personal fulfilment becomes increasingly difficult to achieve as the novel progresses. But I have only gained a hint of this; there is much more work to do before I can make anything of it. Certainly, if I survey my passages chronologically they suggest human continuity but also historical change. Even from a small extract we can sense that Ursula's world is recognisably akin to our own, while the earlier passages show the older Brangwens living in an intense interior way, more insulated from outside pressures.

I feel I have made quite a lot of progress with *The Rainbow*, but in addition to further examination of the Brangwens, I still have huge areas of the text to explore. I am aware, for example, of many splendid set-pieces of description, such as Will and Anna's stock-gathering under the moon (pp. 159–63), the interior of Lincoln Cathedral (pp. 243–5), or the horses that cause Ursula such distress at the end of the novel (p. 539–42) any adequate reading must accommodate such passages and assess their significance in the overall organisation of the text. More work needs to be done on the obscure struggles between couples that much of *The Rainbow* evolves around, and on why Lawrence spends so much time on them. Finally, Lawrence opens up a more public world of schools, mining towns and university education in the second half of the novel. How does this relate to our theme and what coherence can we find in such apparently random material? These are all questions that are yet to be answered.

II Aspects of the novel

Those who do not like Lawrence's novels very much tend to argue that he spends a disproportionate amount of time dwelling on those moments of intense passion and heightened consciousness that occur between two people involved with each other in a sexual and emotional way, and that, in doing so, he writes in an unnaturally strained and obscure manner. Neither the material he chooses nor the way he writes, they conclude, are conducive or natural to the creation of good fiction. It seems to me that if you have a traditional view of what fiction is and what it is supposed to do, there is a lot of strength in this argument. It is only if you are prepared to let Lawrence shift and alter your assessment of what a novel is and what its capabilities are that you can write about him sympathetically and constructively.

Let us tackle the problem of the oddness of much of the language at *The Rainbow* by examining a passsage:

> They had passed through the doorway into the further space, where movement was so big, that it contained bonds and constraints and labours, and still was complete liberty. She was the doorway to him, he to her. At last they had thrown open the doors, each to the other, and had stood in the doorways facing each other, whilst the light flooded out from behind on to each of their faces, it was the transfiguration, the glorification, the admission. (p. 133)

This seems typically 'Lawrentian' writing in that, read and examined unsympathetically, it begins to look like wordy and bombastic nonsense. How on earth, one might ask, can anyone be 'a doorway' to anyone else and then stand in his/her own doorway, having thrown the door open to the other person? Isn't this business of light flooding out from behind the two people, and the use of words such as 'transfiguration' and 'glorification', rather exaggerated? Why can't he write clearly?

The problem, as I see it, is that Lawrence here, as elsewhere, is stretching language in an attempt to express feelings, moods, intuitions, in fact whole areas of personal experience, that are very difficult to articulate formally and consciously. Bluntly, Lawrence is taking language into areas where language does not go or 'fit' very easily. Language is normally used deliberately and consciously; it is a social discourse with socially accepted meanings, so there will be a sense of strain when Lawrence bends it to express his own private meanings. We have come to expect this strangeness in certain kinds of modern experimental poetry, but we do not expect it in novels, which we think should deal with the normal, the social, or what is generally understood as 'reality'.

Lawrence here is trying to express the feelings of Tom and Lydia after they have suddenly, and mutually, 'discovered' each other in a mood of complete trust and glad wonder, and he attempts to express what a sense of liberation such a discovery brings. This only seems possible through a certain kind of rhetoric, or deliberately heightened mode of address, involving extended or repeated uses of metaphor and other forms of figurative writing. Their mutual feelings of love have created a 'further space' into which they have delivered each other; hence the imaginary doorways. Literally the passage is nonsense, but imaginatively it makes a lot of sense, as does the paradox of being in bonds and yet experiencing a new, exhilarating sense of freedom. The wonder of the discovery is underlined by the 'light' imagery and the religious language of 'transfiguration' and 'glorification'.

I have said that in *The Rainbow* Lawrence is pre-eminently concerned with the issues of personal fulfilment and growth. For him these are only possible for the individual through strenuous and serious involvement with another, generally in the form of marriage. A study of intimate relationships, then, is central to Lawrence's art as a novelist. The usual emphasis of the novel is on the tension between the individual and society, that outer world in which he, or she, has to find a place and as much satisfaction as possible. In Lawrence's novels this often gives way to a tension between *and within* individuals as they seek to find a sense of self through one another. Outer social reality often gives way to this interest in interior, psychological struggle, with important consequences for the shape and organisation of the texts. Let me take another passage to show you what I mean.

> Into the rhythm of his work there came a pulse and a steadied purpose. He stopped, he lifted the weight, he heaved it towards her, setting it as in her, under the moonlight space. And he went back for more. Ever with increasing closeness he lifted the sheaves and swung striding to the centre with them, ever he drove her more nearly to the meeting, ever he did his share, and drew towards her, overtaking her. There was only the moving to and fro in the moonlight, engrossed,

> the swinging in the silence, that was marked only by the splash of sheaves, and silence, and a splash of sheaves. And ever the splash of his sheaves broke swifter, beating up to hers, and ever the splash of sheaves recurred monotonously, unchanging, and ever the splash of his sheaves beat nearer.
>
> Till at last, they met at the shock, facing each other, sheaves in hand. And he was silvery with moonlight, with a moonlit, shadowy face that frightened her. She waited for him.
>
> 'Put yours down,' she said.
>
> 'No, it's your turn.' His voice was twanging and insistent.
>
> She set her sheaves against the shock. He saw her hands glisten among the spray of grain. And he dropped his sheaves and he trembled as he took her in his arms. (pp. 161–2)

So what is this about? To say that it is about two people stacking sheaves is rather to miss the point, isn't it? Yet it is possible to respond to the passage, especially its rhythm, without being very clear what is going on or why the passage is there. The temptation is to say that it is very 'poetic' and leave it at that, but that is not enough. It seems to me that the stacking of the sheaves is really an extended metaphor for something else: Will is reaching out for Anna emotionally and this need is objectified in the rhythms of the work. This passage is part of an elaborate set-piece which dramatises Will's wish to subdue Anna to his will, her resistance, and her final yielding to him. Will has a desire, at first unclear to himself, to bring Anna and himself together at the centre of the field, to ensure that they meet, and he adapts the rhythm of his work to this end. His gathering purpose is expressed in phrases such as 'setting it as in her' and 'ever he drove her more nearly to the meeting'.

The hypnotic repetitions of words and whole phrases remind one of the opening passage of the novel describing the Brangwen men; as there, conscious intellectual judgement is lulled into suspension. The reader is caught up in an expression of instinctive need: 'and ever the splash of his sheaves beat nearer'. As both lovers become subdued to a power beyond themselves, so their individual, social identities dissolve into impersonal desire. The dark and the moonlight assume a symbolic potency as the matters of the day give way to the desires of the night. Will is transfigured by the moonlight into something strange and alarmingly challenging for Anna. She has been drawn into this sensuous intimate world and must yield to it.

As so often in these splendid lyrical passages, human desire becomes impersonal as it accords with the forces of nature. Will and Anna are helping to harvest the grain but they are also bringing their courtship to fruition: the scene concludes with Will's proposal. Human desire falls into the larger rhythms of nature, which are seen as magical, strange, enormously powerful, though you need to read the whole episode to get a full sense of this. For Lawrence, 'falling in love' is a venture into the unknown, sometimes exhilarating, sometimes frightening and destructive. You might like to compare this scene with Tom's earlier wooing of Lydia or the way in which Ursula and Anton Skrebensky later manipulate each other's emotions in a similar moonlight scene (pp. 367–9). In such poetic set-pieces Lawrence is finding symbolic external landscapes for interior psychological struggles or states of mind. Such scenes are 'unrealistic' in a conventional sense, being rather operatic as characters act out their needs or dramatise their problems in an extreme or exaggerated way: look at Anna's pregnant dance (p. 225) or Ursula's confrontation with the horses at the end of the book (pp. 539–42). There is a genuine doubt in the latter example as to whether the horses are real or not. But it doesn't really matter. The important thing to grasp is that the horses are a symbol of a repressed part of Ursula's nature; they force her to confront herself and express a state of personal crisis and breakdown.

In a famous letter to Edward Garnett in June 1914, referring to what was to become *The Rainbow*, Lawrence wrote, 'You mustn't look in my novel for the old stable ego of the character,' and 'again I say, don't look for the development of this novel to follow the lines of certain characters: the characters fall into the form of some other rhythmic form'. I take it that by 'the old stable ego of the character' Lawrence meant that sense of character as something stable, solid, socially formed and developed through social interaction. Most novelists and their readers took this view of character before Lawrence, and novels were devised with appropriate plots to draw out and develop characters in this external, social way. In the harvest scene I have discussed, and others that I have mentioned, this 'old stable ego of the character' dissolves; instead the characterisation falls into 'some other rhythmic form'. Clearly Lawrence's more internal view of character will have consequences for the way the text is organised overall. It is to a consideration of the novel's rhythmic form that I now wish to move.

I have mentioned Lawrence's interest in moments of consciousness so intense that they seem to move outside the normal constraints of time. How, though, is it possible to adapt the narrative organisation of the novel to accommodate so many of these 'timeless' moments? The novel, after all, is the literary form that, above all others, pretends to be most like the real world, in particular in its treatment of time. Characters in novels move through an imaginary world that is recognisably akin to our world; this is part of the pleasure of reading fiction, and consequently novels are subject to time. They have to adapt and evolve with it, as we have to in the real world, and, if your initial reading of *The Rainbow* was anything like mine, you were probably frustrated by the way your expectations of 'story' and forward-moving narrative was constantly being balked by yet another intense lyrical or dramatic passage, apparently suspended, outside time. To get the best out of reading Lawrence you have to adjust and adapt your expectations of narrative form. In *The Rainbow* Lawrence endeavours to capture those moments of timeless significance in time by evolving a more cyclical form for his novel, forcing us to range forward and backward, gathering meaning, as we go. Each new experience we encounter draws along with it memories of the past, of previous similar experiences. Lawrence works by parallel and contrast all the time, both in the broader sweeps of his narrative – two childhoods, three courtships, the emotional trials and tribulations of three consummated adult relationships – and in the finer details. I have mentioned the obvious parallel between Will and Anna's nocturnal sheaf-gathering and an analogous moonlit scene when Ursula 'destroys' Anton Skrebensky in the stockyard (pp. 360–9), but there also seems to be another pair of parallel scenes. Will's rhythmic wooing of Anna reminds me of Tom's consoling of Anna when a distraught child by carrying her up and down the lamplit barn feeding the animals (pp. 115–16). Both these scenes refer us back to the timeless, sensuous rhythms of the Brangwen men as they serve nature in the opening section of the novel. So it is that key scenes act as nodal points radiating their significance outwards, helping to give shade and pattern to a text that lacks 'plot' in the usual sense. It is by drawing the significance of such scenes together that we begin to draw conclusions, create meaning, from the text.

We are further helped in this by Lawrence's use of symbolism both as a co-ordinating device and as a means of expressing the inexpressible. We have already seen this at work in the 'doorway' passage with which I opened this section. In fact, Lawrence punctuates this text with frequent references to doorways and archways, especially at the beginning and end of each new set of relationships. This ties in with the theme of journeying and growth I mentioned earlier. In the 'doorway' passage Tom and Lydia make an archway for each other; they meet in 'the span of the heavens' at the end of chapter 3 (p. 134). The other Brangwens are not so fortunate. Anna relinquishes her adventure into the unknown: instead, 'she was a door and a threshold, she herself' (p. 238) for her daughter, while her husband learns that his beloved cathedral doorway was 'no doorway. It was too narrow' (p. 248). Ursula expects the most, so in her dark moods she is the most disillusioned: 'Always the shining doorway ahead; and then upon approach, always the shining doorway was a gate into another ugly yard, dirty and active and dead' (p. 487).

Such recurring symbolism helps us to make significant distinctions between the Brangwen generations and their attitude to life. It is not simply ornamental or decorative, but part of a process by which Lawrence enforces structural coherence on a plotless narrative.

The rainbow itself is, of course, Lawrence's central symbol, gathering meaning as the text moves along. Just how successful it is you must judge for yourself, but it is easy to see why Lawrence is drawn to it as an image of visionary possibilities, because it reconciles elements that everywhere else in life are held apart: earth, air, fire and water. This is the magic that the rainbow has always had, but Lawrence adapts a powerful traditional symbolism for his own purposes. For him, I think, it becomes the symbol of the elusive dream of perfected relationships towards which we must always strive, or give up our humanity. By the end of the book it has broadened still further to become a secularised vision of the Old Testament covenant, symbol of hope in the new, dark, industrial days. This rather surprising notion of the Industrial Revolution as a modern equivalent of the Flood, with Ursula as a latter-day Noah brings me to a consideration of the public world of the novel and Lawrence's treatment of history and social themes.

So far in this section I have chosen to emphasise Lawrence's interest in extreme states of psychological drama or tension, and how he slows the narrative down to accommodate them.

However, if this was all that he was interested in, then strictly speaking he would be writing not novels but extended prose poems. A forward-moving narrative is essential to any novel. Novels, as I have said, create characters who exist in time, and novels, however sophisticated, tell stories. *The Rainbow* is no exception. Lawrence may delve deeper into the subconscious than most novelists, but he is also interested in social identity and social interaction: indeed, *The Rainbow* has been praised as an invaluable record of provincial life and Lawrence as a fine, perceptive social historian.

How can this be when so much of the novel is inward-looking and evolves around so few characters? Besides, as we have seen, very little seems to 'happen' to these characters that we could count as 'history'. It all seems so private and personal.

The answer lies, I think, in seeing that Lawrence's radical interest in complex interior psychological states leads him to fresh insights into the tension between the individual and society, a tension which he rewrites as a conflict between the individual's sense of 'being' and the various exterior roles that society seeks to impose on him or her, sometimes with destructive consequences. Paradoxically, it is by going so deeply into his characters in a psychological way that Lawrence is able to mount such a fresh and challenging social critique. It is true, though, that Lawrence only really begins to explore this social dimension in the second half of his novel, and pre-eminently with the character of Ursula.

I have said that novels tell stories. At a personal level *The Rainbow* tells how three generations of Brangwens seek to discover their potential in life, but their struggles are part of and demonstrate a much grander story: namely, the transformation of English society in the second half of the nineteenth century. Before 1840 less than half the population lived in towns; by 1902, the novel's concluding year, approximately 80 per cent of the population lived in towns and cities. This shift from country to city, from community to individualism, is the novel's social subject and is a hugely ambitious one. It is *the* central experience of the mass of people during this historical period, and the struggles of the Brangwens must be placed and studied in this context.

How can such a massive and complex social changes be encompassed and studied in a fiction? Well, partly in the time-honoured way of charting the destinies of individual characters. Tom Brangwen stays where he is; Will moves from lace-designing to art-teaching; Ursula cuts free from her family to become a teacher, a university student and an emancipated woman. In this way, Lawrence can dramatise the accelerating changes within society. The open, inconsequential nature of Ursula's progress through the second half of the novel is a dramatisation of what it is like to make one's way in this new urban world where one's sense of self enters into conflict with a number of roles that society imposes on you. Thus Ursula's image of herself as a sensitive, caring individual is contradicted by the need to become an efficient teacher if her emancipation is to be allowed to continue. Her conformity in one role is the price that society exacts for the greater freedom she enjoys in other areas of her life. There is loss and gain in the breakdown of community, and Lawrence was very aware of this from his own experience. His treatment of eduction in this novel will repay careful examination, as it ties the personal and the social very neatly together. It is necessary for individual growth – remember the Brangwen women looking outward from their farms in the opening section – but it is also essential for upward mobility in the new society.

However, analysis at the level of character alone will not do justice to the range and comprehensiveness of Lawrence's social vision. The Brangwens are not 'case-histories' and Lawrence is not a social historian working out a complex thesis through painstaking research, but an imaginative novelist seeking to embody an intuitively felt set of truths about modern life in a 'fiction' – a crafted piece of extended writing subject to its own laws. We must never make the mistake of assuming that a novel is a simple window on the world. Let us look at Lawrence's description of Wiggiston, the mining town where the young Tom Brangwen is a manager.

> The place had the strange desolation of a ruin. Colliers hanging about in gangs and groups, or passing along the asphalt pavements heavily to work, seemed not like living people, but like spectres. The rigidity of the blank streets, the homogenous amorphous sterility of the whole suggested death rather than life. There was no meeting place, no centre, no artery, no organic formation. There it lay, like the new foundations of a red-brick confusion rapidly spreading, like a skin-disease. (p. 393)

This is Ursula's view of the town, but it does seem to have the author's tacit approval. What strikes me is Lawrence's refusal here to penetrate imaginatively the full complexity of a miner's life or modern urban living conditions. His view is entirely negative. The modern industrial world is seen as a machine and its inhabitants are reduced to ghosts or automata. When Lawrence does think organically, it is only to see modern urban development as some hideous disease proliferating like a cancer. Now, this is very powerful writing but it isn't history – it's myth. Lawrence here is contributing to a prevalent modern myth of the city as 'wasteland' or hell. In fact the whole book deals with complex, historical realities – the shift from a rooted, agrarian society to an industrial, urban one – mythically. It is only through myth that Lawrence could interpret and express the conflict and contradictory emotions that modern progress evoked in him. The myths that he uses and that provide the sub-text to his story, deepening and elaborating it, are those that his readers would immediately and intuitively respond to – namely, the old Bible stories. Everywhere in this novel there is the calculated use of religious language, metaphors and analogies. In effect, Lawrence is rewriting the Old Testament for the new, secular age. Your grasp of the novel will be greatly enhanced if you can understand this aspect of Lawrence's method. Lawrence was a passionately religious man, not in the sense of being a believer in a creed but in his commitment to life and living fully. Giving a significance to moments in ordinary lives by giving them a religious notation comes very naturally to him, so the Brangwens become Old Testament patriarchs, their struggles those of the Israelites searching out the Promised Land. Will and Anna's honeymoon is blessed by a nativity carol (p. 182); Anna dances 'before the Lord' in the fullness of her pregnancy (p. 225); Ursula becomes a prophetess crying in the wilderness of modern society.

I have suggested that Lawrence's feelings towards industrial society and the progress that it brings were very ambiguous: at one level it diminishes our capacity for 'life' – we can see this very clearly in the Wiggiston passage just quoted – yet at another it provides the necessary conditions for the personal fulfilment so important for Lawrence. Ursula's story is, after all, a kind of rewrite of his own early struggles for emancipation. and this is a major source of conflict and tension in the text, a contradiction of meaning that is only partially resolvable through the use of symbol and myth. For example, Marsh Farm is made a kind of pre-industrial Eden by Lawrence; it is the home of instinctual life and 'blood knowledge'. The arrival of the canal, the railway and the pit signal a fall from innocence into a new, more destructive world of mental consciousness. This is very evident in the marital conflict of Will and Anna. Yet Edens are made to be destroyed: Marsh Farm, as the name implies, is sluggish and inert. It is treated with nostalgia but must be left behind. It is both praised yet implicitly condemned. Lawrence has written his own version of the 'fortunate fall' where loss at one level is also a gain at another. Organic 'rootedness' is all very well, but it must be transcended. Each generation aspires outwards in search of the rainbow.

The paradox is further explored in Lawrence's treatment of Ursula. Her career is one of ruthless disassociation from those beings or institutions that seek to tie her down or limit her in some way – her parents, family, college, Winifred, Skrebensky – and this is seen as brave and necessary. Yet at another level we feel obscurely that she is damaging herself and becoming neurotically self-absorbed – so much so that she is brought to a nervous breakdown at the end of the novel. Lawrence seems to have brought himself to an impasse which can only be resolved by the rather arbitrary intervention of the rainbow symbol in the final paragraph, a glowing symbol of hope amid the ugliness of contemporary England.

There is a lot of controversy about the success or failure of the novel's conclusion. I do not want to prejudge the issue. There are arguments on both sides, and, in this as in other contentious areas, you will have to assess the evidence and make up your own minds. What I should like to stress is that substantial, imaginative texts aren't tidy: *The Rainbow* is full of tangles and contradictions; this is what makes it so rich and productive of meaning. The critic's job is to expose the issues, not provide easy answers that ignore half the evidence.

The rainbow symbol at the end attempts to transcend the problems that Lawrence himself has expressed in other areas of the text; through Ursula's resilience and faith, he insists on hope through the darkest days. This was a message, though, that Lawrence was not able to sustain in his next major novel, *Women in Love*.

5

Women in Love (1920)

I Constructing an overall analysis

IF YOU have just read *Women in Love* for the first time, you may well be unsure what to make of it. It is the most experimental of Lawrence's novels and represents his most radical break with traditional conventions of novel-writing. Don't let this put you off, however, for it is a great novel, and as you work on it you will come to get hold of its distinctive greatness for yourself. As ever, the best way to start is by constructing a plot synopsis.

1 *After reading the novel, think about the story and what kind of pattern you can see in the text.*

This is my version of events:

> The novel opens at the Brangwen family home in Beldover. Ursula, now a teacher at the local grammar school, discusses marriage with her sister Gudrun, who has just returned from a bohemian life in London. They go to observe a local society wedding and so see the other main characters that are to feature in the novel: Gerald Crich, a mine-owner, whose sister's wedding it is, Rupert Birkin, friend of Gerald and a school inspector, and Hermione Roddice, an aristocratic, intellectual society hostess, who is Birkin's lover.
>
> As the novel progresses, it becomes a story of intense personal relationships and love affairs. Though of lower class than the Criches and the Roddices, the Brangwen sisters are invited to their houses and become part of their social set. When Birkin's relationship with Hermione finally collapses, he marries Ursula after a complex, tempestuous courtship. She cuts her family ties, they both resign their jobs and determine to seek a new life together outside society.

Gerald is a powerful, successful industrialist, but his private life is dogged by tragedy and misfortune. Gudrun admires Gerald's domineering personality and he, in turn, becomes more and more reliant on her. He engages her as an art tutor to his youngest sister and, on his father's death, she becomes his mistress.

Counterpointing these two love affairs is the close, emotional bond between Gerald and Birkin: this is more demonstrative on Birkin's side, as he is searching for some permanent male attachment to complement his sexual love for Ursula, but it is important to them both.

The novel ends with the removal of both pairs of lovers from the Midland industrial scene that has provided the setting for most of the narrative to a remote hotel in the Austrian Tyrol where they go for a holiday together. Here Gudrun falls under the spell of a decadent German artist, Loerke, and her relationship with Gerald rapidly deteriorates. Discomforted, Ursula and Birkin leave for Italy and, in their absence, Gerald, after attempting to strangle Gudrun in a jealous rage, dies from exposure by walking into the snow alone. The novel ends with Birkin mourning his dead friend and the loss of a love that Ursula cannot provide.

I must confess I found it quite difficult to condense the book in this way. And my account itself seems inadequate and only moderately useful, unlike the similar synopses I have made for *Sons and Lovers* and *The Rainbow*. These did give me some insight into the organisation of the novels in a way that this seems not to; it does not do justice to the diversity of the novel's episodes or the complexity of its organisation. Give or take a few unusual features such as the friendship between Gerald and Birkin or the inconclusive, unhappy ending, this could be the synopsis for any popular romantic fiction. In other words, the story is about rather glamorous people in high society who fall in and out of love with each other and appear to do very little else. But this disappointing disparity between the rich confusion of the reading experience and the abstracted summary of the novel's events can, in itself, tell us a great deal. In a negative way it informs us that, in our search for structure and organisation, the 'plot', such as it is, is not going to be particularly helpful. Part of the undoubted difficulty of the book is the disparity between the events that occur, often rather trivial or private, and the enormous significance that Lawrence chooses to attach to them. The plot of the romantic love story is distorted out of all recognition by Lawrence's extensive analysis of individual psychology and his examination of modern industrial society.

This is an important step forward, for, if we can see that Lawrence is subverting the form of love novelette, this also means he is subverting and questioning the whole notion of 'love' that that particular form of novel-writing underpins and supports. In some sense 'love' is the subject of *Women in Love*, as the title suggests, but we are already aware that 'love' is not a simple, romantic concept. Even the most impressionistic first reading tells us that this is a double love story involving two sisters; one ends badly, the other more or less well, but neither conforms to the orthodoxies of conventional love affairs as depicted in popular romantic fiction. My first steps towards making a basic analysis must be to map out the process of these love affairs and attempt to make distinctions between them.

2 *Select a short passage featuring one of the main characters and try to build upon the ideas you have established so far*

We need a passage close to the beginning of the novel to get us started. Neither of the two major love affairs gets under way for some time, but in the first chapter we are given an analysis of a woman already, and unhappily, 'in love'. This is Hermione Roddice, whom we meet arriving at Willey Green church for the wedding (page references to the novel relate to the Penguin edition, 1982).

> No one could put her down, no one could make mock of her, because she stood among the first, and those that were against her were below her, either in rank, or in wealth, or in high association of thought and progress and understanding. So, she was invulnerable. All her life, she had sought to make herself invulnerable, unassailable, beyond reach of the world's judgement.
>
> And yet her soul was tortured, exposed. Even walking up the path to the church, confident as she was that in every respect she stood beyond all vulgar judgement, knowing perfectly that her appearance was complete and perfect, according to the first standards, yet she suffered a torture, under her confidence and pride, feeling herself exposed to wounds and to mockery and to despite. She always felt vulnerable, vulnerable, there was always a secret chink in

her armour. She did not know herself what it was. It was a lack of robust self, she had no natural sufficiency, there was a terrible void, a lack, a deficiency of being within her.

And she wanted someone to close up this deficiency, to close it up for ever. She craved for Rupert Birkin. When he was there, she felt complete, she was sufficient, whole. For the rest of the time she was established on the sand, built over a chasm, and, in spite of all her vanities and securities, any common maid-servant of positive, robust temper could fling her down this bottomless pit of insufficiency, by the slightest movement of jeering or contempt. And all the while the pensive, tortured women piled up her own defences of aesthetic knowledge and culture, and world-visions, and disinterestedness. Yet she could never stop up the terrible gap of insufficiency. (pp. 63–4)

As before, I shall break down this passage in the usual sequence but without declaring each step explicitly. So what is this passage about? Most obviously it is a direct authorial investigation of Hermione's state of mind as she arrives for the wedding. Her innermost fears and weaknesses are exposed but from the perspective of the third person. Lawrence is rather fond of this indirect mode of narrating and exploring the intimate recesses of his characters' consciousness; it is as if he were inside their heads taking notes. The effect is to make his revelations of his their state of mind at any one time particularly persuasive and authoritative.

The obvious tension in the passage is between Hermione's confident public persona and her inner insecurity. The passage opens by stressing her rank, wealth and culture, yet she is vulnerable. The key phrase seems to be 'a lack of robust self', in the second paragraph. Hermione needs to be self-sufficient, is surrounded by the armour of wealth and privilege, yet is pitiably aware and morbidly conscious of the opinions of others. She needs an essential 'something'; there is a critical deficiency in her sense of identity, a deficiency that she is looking to Birkin to supply.

In this sense 'love' is seen as something morbid and unhealthy, a 'craving' or addiction that is emphasised by the paradoxical metaphors: she is 'established on the sand, built over a chasm' and is pathetically vulnerable to criticism of anyone who has a healthy self-regard. This 'terrible void', this 'terrible gap of insufficiency' is, one feels, unbridgeable, unfillable: Hermione's demands and claims on 'love' are just too much; they have become a substitute for her neurotic lack of self-sufficiency.

The passage itself, it is worth noting, is part of a debate on love and marriage that dominates the first chapter (it opens with the sisters discussing the hazards and pitfalls of marriage), and one suspects that it will form the substance of the novel overall. However, the tone of the opening part of the chapter is very wry, ironic, detached, essentially taut, dramatic dialogue with an undertone of panic and fear. Here, by contrast, we are plunged into an exhaustive interior analysis of 'being in love', and very distressing it is too. Clearly this form of love is a hopeless, degrading dependency, an experience to be avoided.

One final thing strikes me about the passage. The language is extraordinarily aggressive. Hermione's efforts at self-sufficiency are described in terms appropriate to a military campaign. She is 'unassailable', 'invulnerable', 'no one could put her down'. She 'piles up her defences'. On the other hand, she is 'tortured', 'exposed to wounds', has 'a secret chink in her armour' and even feels herself 'flung down bottomless pits'. Again, this hostility and violence seems to be a feature of the opening chapter: one remembers the sisters' attitude to men, their family and society in general, and, maybe, the book as a whole. It is a feature I am alerted to now and must remember to look out for.

3 *Select a second passage for discussion*

I shall move straight on to a passage that deals with one pair of lovers, Ursula and Birkin, at an initial stage in their relationship.

> She heard, but did not notice the click of the door. Suddenly she started. She saw, in a shaft of ruddy, copper-coloured light near her, the face of a man. It was gleaming like fire, watching her, waiting for her to be aware. It startled her terribly. She thought she was going to faint. All her suppressed, subconscious fear sprang into being with anguish.
>
> 'Did I startle you?' said Birkin, shaking hands with her. 'I thought you had heard me come in.'
>
> 'No,' she faltered, scarcely able to speak. He laughed, saying he was sorry. She wondered why it amused him.
>
> 'It is so dark.' he said. 'Shall we have the light?'
>
> And moving aside, he switched on the strong electric lights. The class-room was distinct and hard, a strange place after the soft dim magic that filled it before he came. Birkin turned curiously to look at Ursula. Her eyes were round and wondering, bewildered, her mouth quivered slightly. She looked like one who is suddenly wakened. There was a living, tender beauty, like a tender light of dawn shining from her face. He looked at her with a new pleasure, feeling gay in his heart, irresponsible.

> 'You are doing catkins?' he asked, picking up a piece of hazel from a scholar's desk in front of him.
>
> 'Are they as far out as this? I hadn't noticed them this year.' He looked absorbedly at the tassel of hazel in her hand.
>
> 'The red ones too!' he said, looking at the flickers of crimson that came from the female bud.
>
> Then he went in among the desks, to see the scholar's books. Ursula watched his intent progress. There was a stillness in his motion that hushed the activities of her heart. She seemed to be standing aside in arrested silence, watching him move in another concentrated world. His presence was so quiet, almost like a vacancy in the corporate air.
>
> Suddenly he lifted his face to her, and her heart quickened at the flicker of his voice:
>
> 'Give me some crayons, won't you?' he said, 'so that they can make the gynaecious flowers red and the androgynous yellow. I'd chalk them in plain, chalk in nothing else, merely the red and yellow. Outline scarcely matters in this case. There is just the one fact to emphasise.' (pp. 84–5)

This is the first meeting of Ursula and Birkin in the novel and we see them in their professional capacities as teacher and school inspector. Though the substance of Birkin's speech is professional, we are made aware that their interest in each other goes beyond the class-room. Birkin uses his privileges to assert his authority as a male as well as a school inspector. His brutal intrusion into her world is both physical and mental; there is something predatory in his manner of stalking her and then enjoying her discomforture. By turning on the electric lights, he sharply 'awakens' her out of her reverie and twilight world. I feel the gesture has metaphorical significance; it is as if he awakens her emotionally, revealing her vulnerability, her 'tender light', and this excites his interest. The 'point of view' or narrative perspective in the passage is very mobile; we begin with Ursula's sudden awareness of his presence, move to his gathering awareness of her startled beauty, and then return to Ursula's view of him at work in the classroom. This constant shifting of viewpoint has the effect of drawing us into the encounter, experiencing it more intimately from both sides.

Some of the sentences and phrases could well have come from conventional romantic fiction. Ursula 'falters' in his presence, 'scarcely able to speak'; the dawn 'shines' from her face, her eyes are 'round and wondering', her mouth 'quivers'. But this rapturous language is qualified by that sense of fear and aggression that

I noted in the first passage. Birkin appears like an apparition and his face gleams 'like fire'. Ursula is 'terribly startled', even believes she might faint as fear 'springs into being' with 'sudden anguish'. Birkin, on the other hand, is amused, envious and 'irresponsibly' enjoying his power over her. Such extremes of feeling are bewildering, even in a love story. I sense strong forces precariously kept in check beneath the superficial social pleasantries.

The chapter which this extract is taken from is called 'Class-Room', an appropriate setting for an educational experience that seems to have nothing to do with Ursula's pupils; they fade into the background. Instead the focus shifts from the human interaction to the catkins and buds of the hazel tree. They are 'the one fact to emphasize'. The technical language that Birkin employs 'gynaecious' and 'androgynous' – should not disguise their function and purpose. They are the hazel tree's sexual organs; it is by the fertilisation of the female buds by the male catkins that the tree comes into leaf and fresh growth every spring. Birkin seems to have a complex double role in this extract. On one hand he is commenting on the facts of nature, showing both appreciation and proper scientific respect for the facts and the need to teach them correctly. At quite another level, he is a participant in nature's drama and design himself. It would seem he has 'quickened' Ursula into new and painful growth – 'she looked like one who is suddenly wakened' – just as the yellow catkin will quicken the red buds into fresh leaf. The repetition of the word 'flicker' to describe both the female hazel buds and Birkin's voice seems to underline the correspondence between the two events. Ursula seems mesmerised by Birkin as he goes about his business, and both are caught up in a process of mutual attraction that has nothing to do with conscious decision or will.

4 *Select a third passage for discussion*

> Gudrun reached out the sketch-book, Gerald stretched from the boat to take it. And as he did so, he remembered Gudrun's last words to him, and her face lifted up to him as he sat on the swerving horse. An intensification of pride went over his nerves, because he felt in some way she was compelled by him. The exchange of feeling between them was strong and apart from their consciousness.

> And as if in a spell, Gudrun was aware of his body, stretching and surging like the marsh-fire, stretching towards her, his hand coming straight forward like a stem. Her voluptuous, acute apprehension of him made the blood faint in her veins, her mind went dim and unconscious. And he rocked on the water perfectly, like the rocking of phosphorescence. He looked round at the boat. It was drifting off a little. He lifted the oar to bring it back. And the exquisite pleasure of slowly arresting the boat, in the heavy-soft water, was complete as a swoon. (pp. 179–80)

I have chosen this passage from chapter 10, 'Sketch-Book', as a parallel and contrast to the previous one. This, too, shows two potential lovers becoming sharply aware of each other. What I need to discover is whether the passage will reveal significant differences that will help me evaluate and distinguish between the two sisters and their lovers. The immediate context is that Gudrun has been sketching some water-plants that particularly fascinate her by the edge of Willey Water when Gerald rows Hermione towards her and Hermione asks to see the sketchbook. These two paragraphs record the impressions and sensations of the two as the sketchbook is exchanged. Obviously the tension in the passage is the 'exchange of feelings' between Gudrun and Gerald that accompanies the passing of the book. I note the same mobility of perspective as featured in the last passage. We have privileged access into Gerald's feelings in the first paragraph; there is a shift to Ursula at the beginning of the second and a move back to Gerald before the end.

My first impression is that this passage is even more obscure and complex in meaning than the last one. Lawrence writes of the exchange of feeling 'apart from their consciousness' and, in order to express this, he has to write in an extremely oblique and highly figurative manner. As we have noted, it is a technique adopted by Lawrence in *The Rainbow*, but it is even more marked and exaggerated in *Women in Love*, where he goes even further in his attempt to express obscure modes of feeling that are resistant to normal expression.

It is not the first paragraph that provides these difficulties; that seems clear enough. Gudrun's 'last words' referred to here are 'I should think you're proud', which she shouted in anger when witnessing Gerald's ill-treatment of a horse in the previous chapter (p. 171). That was a scene which had both shocked and obscurely excited her by its demonstration of power and will.

Gerald here senses her fascination and it excites him. But the second paragraph is altogether more strange and ambiguous. I said that Usula was mesmerised by Birkin in the last passage, here Gudrun seems to go a stage further. She appears to have some kind of surrealist vision or intuition into Gerald's inner being that is both exciting and menacing. It is very difficult to paraphrase such writing, but I sense that Gudrun is responding to something fascinatingly degenerate in Gerald. He is akin to the marsh-plants she is sketching; like them he emerges from the marshy water, his reaching hand 'like a stem'. In a very odd simile he is seen as 'stretching and surging' like the marsh-fire. Marsh-fire is the product of rotting vegetation, known proverbially as 'will-o'-the-wisp' or, to give it its Latin tag, *Ignis fatuus*, 'the flame that deceives'. In folklore, will-o'-the-wisp lures unwary travellers to their destruction. It seems to follow that Gerald is apprehended by Gudrun as some kind of spectre of corruption possessed of a beguiling but deceitful appearance. This is in contrast with the Usula–Birkin passage where there was a much more objective play of interest. Birkin had an interest in Usula, it is true, but was able to move into a more detached role when observing the catkins or discussing teaching methods. In comparison, this encounter seems unhealthily self-absorbed, both characters savouring their excitement and pleasure in a manner I feel is rather sinister. The hazel catkins and buds were a robust kind of symbolism, clear and distinct from man, with an emphasis on growth. Gerald's association with the marsh-plants is altogether more introverted and confusing, compelling yet corrupt. The vocabulary is strongly erotic: 'voluptuous, acute apprehension', 'faint', 'dim and unconscious', 'rocked . . . perfectly', 'rocking', 'drifting', 'exquisite pleasure', 'slowly arresting', 'heavy-soft', 'swoon'. My response to such language is very mixed. While at one level the emphasis on pleasure is difficult to resist, the hypnotic quality of the writing, lulling the conscious mind to sleep, makes me uneasy. Lawrence is supposed to insist on the need for letting go of conscious control in emotional relationships as a good and necessary thing, but this is not the sense I get from this passage, partly because the writing seems over-insistent, and partly because Gerald is associated with rotting vegetation and the deceptive glow – 'phosphorescence' – of marsh-fire. This relationship, Lawrence seems to be suggesting, has its origins in decay. You may disagree, and you are entitled to, for Lawrence makes no clear moral judgement on the matter. I think you will agree, though, that the writing is very ambiguous.

5 *Select a fourth passage for discussion*

By looking at two early passages that deal with the lovers at the very onset on their relationships, I have got some ideas or intuitions to follow up. It seems that the very best way forward would be to examine two later passages to see how these affairs develop.

> 'You want the paradisal unknowing,' she said, turning round on him as he still sat half visible in the shadow. 'I know what that means, thank you. You want me to be your thing, never to criticize you or to have anything to say for myself. You want me to be a mere *thing* to you! No, thank you! *If* you want that, there are plenty of women who will lie down for you to walk over them – *go* to them then, if that's what you want – go to them.'
>
> 'No,' he said, outspoken with anger. 'I want you to drop your assertive *will*, your frightened apprehensive self-insistence, that is what I want. I want you to trust yourself so implicity that you can let yourself go.'
>
> 'Let myself go!' she re-echoed in mockery. 'I can let myself go easily enough. It is you who can't let yourself go, it is you who hang on to yourself as if it were your only treasure. *You* – *you* are the Sunday school teacher – *you* – you preacher!'
>
> The moment of truth that was in this made him stiff and unheeding of her.
>
> 'I don't mean let yourself go in the Dionysic ecstatic way,' he said. 'I know you can do that. But I hate ecstasy, Dionysic or any other. It's like going round in a squirrel cage. I want you not to care about yourself, just to be there and not to care about yourself, not to insist – be glad and sure and indifferent.'
>
> 'Who insists?' she mocked. 'Who is it that keeps on insisting? It isn't *me*!'
>
> There was a weary, mocking bitterness in her voice. He was silent for some time.
>
> 'I know,' he said 'While ever either of us insists to the other, we are all wrong. But there we are, the accord doesn't come.'
>
> They sat in stillness under the shadow of the trees by the bank. The night was white around them, they were in the darkness, barely conscious.
>
> Gradually, the stillness and peace came over them. She put her hand tentatively on his. Their hands clasped softly and silently in peace. (pp. 327–8)

This is a lover's quarrel from chapter 19, 'Moony', an important turning-point for Ursula and Birkin, for at the end of the chapter, after she leaves him, he resolves to marry her. As the passage is about a quarrel, it is not difficult to see where the tension lies. There is a conflict between their differing definitions of love and how they wish each other to be. Ursula thinks that Birkin wants her to be a passive object, a simple gratification of his desire. She finds him obsessively preoccupied with himself and his needs and so unable to respond to her simply and directly. He feels that her demands, like Hermione's, come from a nagging, fearful lack of self-sufficiency. He believes that, if they could just leave each other alone and trust in themselves, it would all come right. There is a sense in which they both see the justice in the other's case, though Birkin is the one who acknowledges it. It is in the silence after the angry words that the reconciliation comes.

My first impression after the last extract is how articulate this pair of lovers are in defining their needs and resentments. With Gerald and Gudrun we were in a world of intimation and intuition, deep in their interior consciousnesses as Lawrence sought to express the pre-verbal and inarticulate. Here we see a very different set of skills; Lawrence has great abilities as a dramatist and a wonderful ear for the rhythms of spoken language. People repeat themselves when excited, and the argument is built up out of skilful repetition of words and phrases: 'You want' (five times), 'I want' (four times), 'plenty of women' (twice), 'thank you' (twice), 'thing' (twice), 'go to them' (twice), 'let go' (five times), 'it is you' (twice), 'you' (four times in ten words), 'insist' (four times), 'not to care about yourself' (twice). When people argue they tend to pick up words and phrases from each other and throw them back again. Lawrence catches this backward and forward motion very well: 'You want' and 'I want'; 'You can let yourself go', 'I can let myself go' and 'It is you who can't let yourself go'; 'not to insist' and 'Who insists?'; and so on.

Of course this argument takes place in a novel, not on the stage, but Lawrence does as much as he can to help us *hear* it going on. He italicizes words to give them stress, uses hyphens and exclamation marks to indicate the broken, incomplete nature of speech, especially angry speech, and indicates how some of the phrases should be heard: 'outspoken in anger', 're-echoed in mockery', 'a weary, mocking bitterness in her voice'.

The repetitions I have noticed with their simple insistences are qualified by a complex vocabulary and sophisticated, figurative language that elaborately maps out abstruse areas of feeling with the help of concrete metaphors, similes and personification: 'paradisal unknowing', 'Dionysic ecstatic way', 'like going round in a squirrel cage', 'drop your assertive *will*, your frightened apprehensive self-insistence', 'hang on to yourself as if it were your only treasure'.

Obviously it is not everyone who can mention the Greek god Dionysos so easily in the heat of an argument: this couple are well matched; they are articulate as well as combative, but that is appropriate when one considers their jobs. They are intellectuals, after all. I sense a paradox, however. Such a brilliant display of linguistic skill seems both necessary and futile. It is not language, finally, that can bridge the gap between them. It is only when the shouting stops, in the soothing, silent darkness, that peace and sympathy draw them together. The clasping hands are ultimately more eloquently communicative that words. Still, the effort of verbal communication, the conscious articulation of needs and desires, may be the necessary precondition for such a silent truce and mutual accord.

This extract is part of a debate about 'love', and the need for the right kind of relationships between people, that runs right through *Women in Love*. Indeed, when I think about it, this novel is particularly disputatious and full of talk: arguments and intellectual discussions, vigorous and unresolved debates are a feature throughout – and usually revolve around Birkin. For example, his argument with Ursula here is a continuation of a conflict instigated in 'Mino' (chapter 3) and only partially resolved in 'Excurse' (chapter 23). The novel ends with both of them in the middle of an unresolved, and probably unresolvable, argument about love.

This, then, seems to be a feature of their relationship that distinguishes it from Gerald and Gudrun's. The latter pair relate to each other in 'unspoken' ways; they are intuitive in their needs and understandings; their relationship is not consciously, intellectually, explored and shared. This is not to say that this necessarily implies a perjorative judgement on Lawrence's part, but it does seem to set them apart. There is a need for Ursula and Birkin to get things out into the light, to recognise conflict and paradox – remember Birkin putting on the lights in the 'Class-Room' passage? – while Gudrun and Gerald 'sink' into their mutual attraction, which, in Lawrence's phrase, is 'apart from their consciousness'. I should like, though, to look at another passage dealing with Gerald and Gudrun to see if this is true.

6 *Select a fifth passage for discussion*

> Quickly he pulled off his jacket, pulled loose his black tie, and was unfastening his studs, which were headed each with a pearl. She listened, watching, hoping no one would hear the starched linen crackle. It seemed to snap like pistol-shots.
>
> He had come for vindication. She let him hold her in his arms, clasp her close against him. He found in her an infinite relief. Into her he poured all his pent-up darkness and corrosive death, and he was whole again. It was wonderful, marvellous, it was a miracle. This was the ever-recurrent miracle in his life, at the knowledge of which he was lost in an ecstasy of relief and wonder. And she, subject, received him as a vessel filled with his bitter potion of death. She had no power at the crisis to resist. The terrible frictional violence of death filled her, and she received it in an ecstasy of subjection, in throes of acute, violent sensation.
>
> As he drew nearer to her, he plunged deeper into her enveloping soft warmth, a wonderful creative heat that penetrated his veins and gave him life again. He felt himself dissolving and sinking to rest in the bath of her living strength. It seemed as if her heart in her breast were a second unconquerable sun, into the glow and creative strength of which he plunged farther and farther. All his veins, that were murdered and lacerated, healed softly as life came pulsing in, stealing invisibly into him as if it were the all-powerful effluence of the sun. His blood, which seemed to have been drawn back into death, came ebbing on the return, surely, beautifully, powerfully.
>
> He felt his limbs growing fuller and flexible with life, his body gained an unknown strength. He was a man again, strong and rounded. And he was a child, so soothed and restored and full of gratitude. (pp. 429–30)

This passage describes Gerald's first love-making with Gudrun when he comes to her bed secretly after his father's death. There seems to be a tension or struggle between Gerald's negative desperation that appears violent and aggressive, and a passive regenerative warmth provided by Gudrun. It is a struggle between life (seen to be female) and death (seen to be male) in which death is in some sense exchanged for life.

Again we have that rapid shifting of narrative perspective that seems to be a feature of this novel. The first paragraph gives us an external view of Gerald from Ursula's point of view, but this soon changes to an interior commentary from his. The first paragraph shows us Gerald pulling off his clothes, and with them his superior social advantages; the dinner jacket, black tie and expensive studs, the starched shirt all emphasize this. There's something menacing about the crackling linen and the studs snapping 'like pistol-shots': they seem a prefiguration of the sexual aggression to come. The purposeful verbs in the second paragraph – 'he had come', 'he found in her', 'into her he poured', – emphasize male dominance and control. Gudrun, on the other hand, is all passivity: 'she let him hold her', 'and she, subject, received him', 'she had no power', 'she received it'. The act of love, a life-giving one, is here reversed into an act of death. In a truly horrible image it is seen as a poisoning which gives miraculous relief to the male. Gudrun is merely a vessel 'subject' to Gerald's will. In language that stresses the act as sadistic on his part and masochistic on hers, Gudrun receives Gerald's 'bitter potion of death' in an 'ecstasy of subjection'. Pleasure is indistinguishable from pain, from 'acute, violent sensation'.

The third paragraph is entirely centred on Gerald. Gudrun is reduced to a set of properties; she is creative heat like the 'all-powerful effluence of the sun' or the enveloping warmth of a hot bath in which he 'plunges' or 'sinks'. In an extraordinary blending of the abstract and the concrete, the spiritual with the biological, 'life', like blood, courses back into Gerald's wounded body, healing him, making him whole again. As in the earlier passage featuring these two, Lawrence is pushing language to the very boundaries of coherence to express complex psychological states. The fourth paragraph draws together a paradox implicit throughout. Gerald is once more confirmed in his manhood. He has, after all, come to her for 'vindication', yet he is also weak, dependent and full of gratitude like a small child.

One of the complaints of the early reviews of *Women in Love* was that it was impossible to make any distinctions between the love-making of Birkin and Ursula and that of Gerald and Gudrun. It is true that I could have chosen a passage where Birken is much more brutal in asserting his needs, but I have picked extracts that emphasize a contrast I do feel to be implicit throughout: namely, that, while Birkin and Ursula talk and reflect upon their difficulties, using language to mediate their love-making, Gerald and Gudrun 'sleep-walk' their way into a relationship without examining it or exploring its likely consequences very clearly. It remains profoundly unexamined in the above passage, as it does earlier when they conspire to subjugate the rabbit Bismarck together and feel a 'mutual hellish recognition' (p. 137), and later, in the Tyrol, when they seek to drag each other down. Indeed, their whole affair is heavily determined by Lawrence, hedged around with images of doom and fate. Just before this extract, Gudrun asks Gerald what he wants of her and he replies, 'I come – because I must. Why do you ask?' (p. 429) Gudrun's response is to feel lost and to give way to fate. This is characteristic of their relationship throughout, I feel. See if you can find evidence for (or against) this yourself.

7 *Have I achieved a sufficiently complex sense of the novel?*

Clearly the answer must be no. We have to yet take into account the elaborate social context in which these affairs take place. There are a wide and diverse number of social groups and settings: Gerald's family and home; Hermione's house party; Birkin's London bohemian set; Beldover, the mining town where the sisters live and Gerald lords it as an 'industrial magnate'. The novel contains an ambitious survey of Lawrence's England through a careful examination of these centres of power and influence. We must attempt to seek out a relationship between the turmoil of 'love' a private emotion and this wider social reality. There must be a connection between the two, for lovers do not live in a vacuum, however much they might like to. Other relationships might provide us with clues and information, particularly on the men. Here we should need to consider Birkin's painful extrication from his dead past with Hermione, Gerald's brief but potent liaison with Minette in London, and most importantly, Birkin's friendship with Gerald. The novel could, with equal justice, be called 'Men in Love', couldn't it?

Birkin has often been seen as Lawrence's own spokesman in the novel, and I think we can perceive that he has an important role apart from his relationship with Ursula; he provides a complex, sustained commentary on the state of modern civilisation generally, an elaborate, philosophical analysis of some felt and perceived crisis that finds it most acute expression in intimate personal relationships but is manifest everywhere. A problem that has exercised the critics is whether Lawrence has adequately 'fictionalised' Birkin into a context or merely made him the mouthpiece for a lot of his own obsessions. Inasmuch as our feelings on the matter might well determine our view of the novel as a success or as a failure full of undigested preaching, it is a problem we cannot neglect.

Finally, although we might know the plot in the sense of 'what happens', we have yet to examine how the novel is organised. We may already feel that the novel has a significant 'shape' or structure, apart from the story, but need to develop our sense of what this is and how it is achieved.

So, there is still a lot of work to be done. But we can take heart from the progress we have made so far. By examining a few passages and asking ourselves some very simple questions, we have achieved access into the novel and begun to crack its codes. On the basis of hard evidence, we know much more than we did about the two main love affairs. To summarise we have found that the Gerald and Gudrun relationship is closed and determined, given over to sensation and self-extinction, and that Birkin and Ursula's is open and negotiable, given over to argument and self-exploration. If the tendency of the first is towards destruction and death, and a neat tragic pattern of fatal love, the tendency of the second is to reach out for life in all its bewildering inconsistency. Moreover, in their drift towards death or struggle for life, these relationships may be illustrating two opposing tendencies within society as a whole and, perhaps, all intimate relationships; that may be why Lawrence has chosen to highlight them. Certainly one of the by-products of our careful readings has been a sense of society as sick, full of fear and violence. 'Love', very far from being an escape, is where these social stresses find their most intense and dramatic expression. It is with these important notions in mind that we can move on to consider other aspects of the text.

II Aspects of the novel

So far I have looked at passages that deal with the intimate emotional and sexual feelings of the five major characters. I should like to broaden the discussion now, and I think that is best done by plunging straight into one of Birkin's general diatribes on the state of modern life and society.

> 'I *do* enjoy things – don't you?' she asked.
>
> 'Oh yes! But it infuriates me that I can't get right, at the really growing part of me. I feel all tangled and messed up, and I *can't* get straight anyhow. I don't know what really to *do*. One must do something somewhere.'
>
> 'Why should you always be *doing*?' she retorted. 'It is so plebeian. I think it is much better to be really patrician, and to do nothing but just be oneself, like a walking flower.'
>
> 'I quite agree,' he said, 'if one has burst into blossom. But I can't get my flower to blossom anyhow. Either it is blighted in the bud, or has got the smother-fly, or it isn't nourished. Curse it, it isn't even a bud. It is a contravened knot.'
>
> Again she laughed. He was so very fretful and exasperated. But she was anxious and puzzled. How was one to get out, anyhow. There must be a way out somewhere.
>
> There was a silence, wherein she wanted to cry. She reached for another bit of chocolate paper, and began to fold another boat.
>
> 'And why is it,' she asked at length, 'that there is no flowering, no dignity of human life now?'
>
> 'The whole idea is dead. Humanity itself is dry-rotten, really. There are myriads of human beings hanging on the bush – and they look very nice and rosy, your healthy young men and women. But they are apples of Sodom, as a matter of fact, Dead Sea fruit, gall-apples. It isn't true that they have any significance – their insides are full of bitter, corrupt ash.'
>
> 'But there *are* good people,' protested Ursula.
>
> 'Good enough for the life of today. But mankind is a dead tree, covered with fine brilliant galls of people.'
>
> Ursula could not help stiffening herself against this, it was too picturesque and final. But neither could she help making him go on. (pp. 185–6)

This is just one of many passages I could have chosen where Lawrence uses Birkin as a link between the private lives of individuals and the public world of the novel, in particular the strained relationship between the individual and society in general that is such a marked feature of *Women in Love*.

In almost every novel one can think of, the hero or heroine has difficulties in adjusting to society and has problems to solve in the course of the book. This is the very stuff of most fictional narrative and the outcome can be happy with the main character finding some sort of accommodation or place in society, often through marriage, or unhappy, in which case the character dies or is banished. Usually, in traditional narratives, society is seen as sustaining and permanent, larger and wiser than any individual who has to come to terms with its demands or suffer the consequences.

On the evidence of the above passage, and many like it, I just don't think this is true in *Women in Love*. The passage seems to revolve around two ideas of fulfilment or 'flowering', to use Birkin's own metaphor – one that is natural, wholesome and good, and another that is unwholesome, rotten and bad. Society can no longer sustain life in any traditional, organic sense, according to Birkin; it can only produce decay and corruption. Birkin blames his own inability to get things right 'at the really growing part of me' on society as a whole, and it is a view of modern life that is not contradicted. It may be that Birkin overstates or gets carried away with his own rhetoric. Ursula obviously thinks so – 'it was too picturesque and final' – but nowhere are his gloomy views on society effectively challenged: indeed, the book in its totality strongly endorses them. Society is not seen as something one can change or contribute to if you are Ursula or Birkin. For all the vehemence of their language, they are both very passive and defeatist. They are annoyed that society cannot enable them 'to be' ' – to 'flower' in their own way, responsible only to themselves as 'patricians'. Instead of a healthy interaction between the individual and society, each changing and adapting to embody the needs of the other, there is a void, an absolute rift between private desires and the outer world in which we all have to live. This will have important consequences for the organisation of the novel overall, because traditional narrative patterns and plot mechanisms will not embody or give a shape to this kind of pessimistic view, a view that is most unusual for a novelist.

This is something I should like to return to, but for the moment I want to stay with this passage and examine Birkin's use of metaphorical language. The notion that mankind is 'blighted in the bud' leads on to the gloomy assertion that humanity is 'dry-rotten' and mankind a 'dead tree' producing fruit that looks healthy but is, in fact, 'apples of Sodom . . . Dead Sea fruit, gall-apples . . . full of bitter, corrupt ash'. This rather colourful language is worth closer scrutiny for its implications. Sodom and Gomorrah were, of course, the wicked and corrupt cities by the shore of the Dead Sea, destroyed by God in the Old

Testament narrative. By association, 'apples of Sodom' are both the product and reward of sin, bitter and barren to the taste. 'Gall' can also mean bitter, a poison or irritant, and 'gall-apples' are also false fruit produced by insects infecting the leaves of certain trees with their poison. There is a blend here, then, of the botanical, scientific language we saw Birkin using in 'Class-Room' and a style that is altogether more biblical, colourful and apocalyptic: Ursula does sometimes see him as a 'Sunday school teacher', and here, as elsewhere, Birkin's gloom and doom are mediated and mitigated by Ursula's thoughts and feelings. Her despondency, her anger, her idling with the piece of chocolate paper are the touches by which Lawrence, the novelist, provides a human context for some of Birkin's more inhuman sermons on the deadness of modern life.

It must be said again, however, that, though Birkin's views are distanced, criticised, even parodied and mocked in the novel, they are supported by the style and narrative organisation of the text as a whole. His view of society as moving towards some great apocalyptic disaster is confirmed by the novel's events and outcome, and above all by the way events and psychological states of mind are described by Lawrence himself as storyteller. Birkin and Lawrence do share substantially the same language and attitude of mind. Look at my general description of outer society in the novel and I think you will find this to be so. Beldover is not seen as an actual industrial town in the early twentieth century, squalid and dirty in places no doubt, but full of vitality, with a capacity for growth and change; instead it is seen as a kind of pagan underworld peopled by ghouls who have given themselves over to the power of the machine (p. 174). The London bohemian world of the Pompadour and Halliday's flat is seen as another kind of limbo, an amorphous 'bubble of pleasure (p. 114) that is sexually and morally chaotic. Breadalby is 'a horrible, dead prison' (p. 154); the social and intellectual games played by Hermione's house-party guests are as predictable and ritualised as the moves in a chess game: 'But the game is known, its going on is like a madness, it is so exhausted' (p. 156). Finally, all Lawrence's feelings of nihilism seem to converge in the white, snowy blankness of the Tyrol, which represents a kind of cul-de-sac, literally a 'dead-end' 'This was the centre, the knot, the navel of the world, where the earth belonged to the skies, pure, unapproachable, impassable' (p. 492).

Any vital, creative growth in individuals as distinct from fungoid growth, the product of decay and rottenness, must, it seems, be apart from and uncontaminated by society, Lawrence's art in *Women and Love* is an art of extremes. The outer world is not the complex interactive web of people and institutions subject to conflict and change that we know society to be. Instead it is a threat to the individual, hostile and other, seen only in the mass, or, close to, as a series of grotesque caricatures. Think of the treatment of Herminone, Mrs Crich, Sir Joshua Mattheson, Halliday and Minette, or Loerke, the decadent artist in the Tyrolean hotel. None of these characters is given a 'rounded' human portrait that we can identify with easily. They are all like sinister, mechanical puppets or dolls. On the broader scale, Birkin's references to Sodom and Gomorrah, and other religious references to wholesale apocalypse and destruction that are such a feature of this text, indicate that Lawrence has chosen to reject the complexities of history for the more simple and poetic truths of myth. The doomed love of Gudrun and Gerald is played out very much in these terms. It seems to belong more to the world of primitive ancient tales than to a 'realistic' novel. Gudrun, after all, is the name of a violent and treacherous princess in the old Norse sagas, and in Norse myth Loki (Loerke) is the evil god who engineered the death of the most well-loved of the gods, Balder. At one level Gerald is a ruthless mine-owner, but at another he is indeed portrayed as a Norse god, beautiful and apparently invincible until tragic weaknesses break him apart.

I should now like to examine a passage that centres on Gerald.

> The rabbit made itself into a ball in the air and lashed out, flinging itself into a bow. It really seemed demoniacal. Gudrun saw Gerald's body tighten, saw a sharp blindness come into his eyes.
>
> 'I know these beggars of old,' he said.
>
> The long, demon-like beast lashed out again, spread on the air as if it were flying, looking something like a dragon, then closing up again, inconceivably powerful and explosive. The man's body, strung to its efforts, vibrated strongly. Then a sudden sharp, white-edged wrath came up in him. Swift as lightning he drew back and brought his free hand down like a hawk on the neck of the rabbit. Simultaneously, there came the unearthly abhorrent scream of a rabbit in the fear of death. It made one immense writhe, tore his wrists and his sleeves in a final convulsion, all its belly flashed white in a whirlwind of paws, and then he had slung it round and had it under his arm, fast. It cowered and skulked. His face was gleaming with a smile. (pp. 315–16)

The novel is punctuated by many scenes of violence like this. One of the symptoms of a sick society, it seems, is excessive coercion in relationships, whether between social classes, men and women, or the human and the natural world. In an analogous earlier scene, Gerald dominates his Arab mare, forcing her to stand at a railway crossing as a train goes by (pp. 168–71). Gudrun taunts some Highland cattle and slaps Gerald's face when he rebukes her (pp. 232–7). Hermione brains Birkin with a paperweight in a moment of extreme frustration (pp. 162–4). Minette stabs a young man in the hand (pp. 123–4). Relationships between lovers are often extremely aggressive either verbally or sexually, finally culminating in Gerald's murderous attack on Gudrun (pp. 572–7).

In this passage the rabbit's freedom, its autonomous sense of self, is violated by Gerald's assertion of will. In the power-struggle between them, both man and rabbit are taken out of their natural being in ways that are seen to be perverse and destructive. Both inflict damage on the other. The rabbit is first a 'ball' and then a 'bow'; its frustrated energy transforms it 'demon-like' into a flying dragon and a 'whirlwind of paws' tearing at Gerald's sleeve. The rest of the passage uses language more appropriate to the torture chamber than the handling of a domestic pet. Gerald is similarly possessed by his exertions, predatory in action 'like a hawk' and sadistic in his triumph.

This theme of vital free energy restrained, the domination of the will, is central to *Women in Love*. Gerald does here what he does to his horse, his miners, Minette, and finally attempts but fails to do in his relationship with Gudrun. She, in her turn, is both obscurely excited by Gerald's power, yearning for the victim's place, but also determined to conquer and experience the thrill of control. If you read again chapter 17 ('The Industrial Magnate'), I think you will begin to perceive Gerald's role in linking the private world of the novel – its depiction of emotional struggle – with wider social and industrial concerns. Birkin, as we have noted, is never committed to society. In a sense he is always half in, half out of the novel's action, commenting on the sickness he perceives both in himself and in others. Gerald, on the other hand, is the most perfect product of the modern world, the finest of its 'Dead Sea fruit'. It is this, I think, that gives him such a heroic, 'larger than life' quality; he accepts modern society unquestioningly – indeed, he helps to shape it by his authority, power and love of efficiency – and Lawrence invests him with a particularly deadly glamour.

Birkin does do things, but largely to act out his frustration in theatrically symbolic ways, as when he walks naked through fir trees after his break with Hermione (pp. 164–6) or stones the reflection of the moon in his exasperation with women (pp. 323–5). When I think of Birkin, though, it is primarily as a *voice*, abstract and philosophical mostly, and always theorizing and questioning. Gerald, however, is a great 'doer'; like all tragic protagonists, he acts out the sickness latent in his society and, in his death, becomes its scapegoat.

If Birkin is a voice, Gerald is pure, poetic presentation. I do believe that he is Lawrence's attempt to portray a modern tragic hero and that is why he is associated with so much sinister and doom-ridden imagery. Under the charming social exterior as Gudrun intuitively perceives, 'his totem is the wolf' (p. 61). He has the mark of Cain; death follows him everywhere. He is associated with water, ice and snow, but also electricity and modern industrial power. One of the difficulties for the reader is learning to see him as a 'character' in the social sense and simultaneously appreciate his role as the 'inhuman' force within society, 'the God of the machine' (p. 301) leading it towards self-destruction.

I said earlier that *Women in Love* could, with equal justice, be called 'Men in Love', and an important aspect of the text is Birkin's relationship with Gerald and whether he can save Gerald from himself. By breaking with Hermione, Birkin is attempting to free himself from a whole mental attitude to life that he perceives as dehumanising and death-directed. It may be a necessary process for society as a whole to go through – society, in a sense, must die before any radical change is possible – but Birkin wishes to escape if he can. 'Love' may be the answer. Through committed personal relationships exceptional men and women may find the means to reconstitute themselves and create meaning from the moral and emotional chaos of the modern world. 'Love', however, does not mean the discredited emotions and expectations of society at large, and a lot of space in this novel is given over to an exploration and attempted redefinition of this term. This can seem boring and repetitive, but it represents a point of fundamental inquiry for Lawrence: in a world hurtling towards destruction, what must I do to be saved?

Birkin is a complex character; his loyalties are unusually torn and these conflicts over the definition of love remain largely unresolved. The love debate, like the wider one on the state of society as a whole, is conducted through a mixture of demonstration and argument. In chapter 13 ('Mino'), when Birkin's tom-cat asserts his authority over a female stray, Birkin uses the incident as a demonstration of his theories, and yet, as Ursula is quick to see, it can also be used to undermine them. Let us look at a passage from the incident:

> 'It is just like Gerald Crich with his horse – a lust for bullying – a real *Wille zur Macht* [will to power] – so base, so petty.'
>
> 'I agree that the *Wille zur Macht* is a base and petty thing. But with the Mino, it is the desire to bring this female cat into a pure stable equilibrium, a transcendent and abiding *rapport* with the single male. Whereas without him, as you see, she is a mere stray, a fluffy sporadic bit of chaos. It is a *volonté de pouvoir* if you like, a will to ability, taking *pouvoir* as a verb.'
>
> 'Ah – ! Sophistries! It's the old Adam.'
>
> 'Oh yes. Adam kept Eve in the indestructible paradise, when he kept her single with himself, like a star in its orbit.'
>
> 'Yes – yes – ' cried Ursula, pointing her finger at him. 'There you are – a star in its orbit! A satellite – a satellite of Mars – that's what she is to be! There – there – you've given yourself away! You want a satellite, Mars and his satellite! You've said it – you've said it – you've dished yourself!'
>
> He stood smiling in frustration and amusement and irritation and admiration and love. She was so quick, and so lambent, like discernible fire, and so vindictive, and so rich in her dangerous flamy sensitiveness. (p. 213)

Now, this is fairly abstract stuff and there's a lot of it in this novel. I think it helps if we do not attempt to make a coherent philosophical position out of such passages. Instead we should view Lawrence as attempting to open up a whole set of unresolvable problems rather than pursuing a thesis. Be suspicious of critics who seek to make Lawrence into too systematic a thinker; he is working in a series of dramatised fictional contexts and his ideas cannot be extracted from these without distortion.

The fundamental paradox here is that Birkin is preaching the need for autonomy in relationships in an extremely partisan, authoritarian way that reveals his need to dominate and control. The manner in which he plays teacher with the French language is typical of his general bossiness, and his view of the stray female without a mate as 'a fluffy sporadic bit of chaos' reveals a rather disparaging view of the female sex in general. Fortunately, Ursula is far too intellectual and independent to be impressed or cowed. Birkin's intellectual use of a metaphor from physics to express the ideal relationship in terms of two masses exerting equal gravitational pull on each other – 'pure stable equilibrium' – soon slips under Ursula's goading into a more traditional notion of the strong male, like a star, exerting his control over a satellite woman. Another paradox is that being caught out in his bullying increases Birkin's love for Ursula as well as his irritation with her. Thus the behaviour of the cats that instigated this debate does not seem an adequate model for the more complex needs of men and women.

Whatever the theory, the reference to Adam and Eve reminds us that sexual love often involves a power-struggle and the tendency for one partner to attempt domination over the other. Despite her vigilance and pride, don't we see Ursula becoming more subservient to Birkin as the novel draws to its conclusion? She does want to yield herself up to Birkin and yet also to own him, possess him for herself. Birkin fears this tendency and where it leads – back into society. After all, marriage is a *social* pact, the point where our personal needs and social claims most intimately fuse. At the beginning of the novel ('In the Train') Birkin proclaims to Gerald his need for a 'sort of ultimate marriage' (p. 110), yet he also wants to break free from society and social validation of his relationships. This a profound contradiction, a split between individual and society that the characters may endlessly debate but which the text can never resolve.

At this point in my analysis of the novel's broader significance I should like to look at another passage:

> So they wrestled swiftly, rapturously, intent and mindless at last, two essential white figures working into a tighter closer oneness of struggle, with a strange, octopus-like knotting and flashing of limbs in the subdued light of the room; a tense white knot of flesh gripped in silence between the walls of old brown books. Now and again came a sharp gasp of breath, or a sound like a sigh, then the rapid thudding of movement on the thickly-carpeted floor, then the strange sound of flesh escaping under flesh. Often, in the white interlaced knot of violent living being that swayed silently, there was no head to be seen, only the swift, tight limbs, the solid white backs, the physical junction of two bodies clinched into oneness. (p. 349)

This is another piece of poetic presentation, more akin to the rabbit passage than to Birkin's argument with Ursula. Birkin sought to define 'equilibrium' through intellectual definition: here it is silently and dramatically acted out, a naked struggle of competing energies on the carpet of a book-lined room. It is an extraordinary, memorable image, one of many in this novel. One might be forgiven for seeing it as a description of love-making; the language is unmistakably erotic. The wrestlers are rapturously 'intent and mindless' in their struggle, their limbs 'flashing' and 'knotting' together; the only sounds are sighs and gasps, rapid thudding and flesh moving against flesh – bodies 'clinched into oneness'. There is a sense too, though, of the description moving towards the bizarre or abstract. The wrestlers become a kind of strange beast in their 'octopus-like' knotting – a 'white interlaced knot of violent living' that sways silently with 'no head to be seen'.

In comparison with the rabbit passage, there is no winner here, no dominance, but a strange collaboration and partnership. Gerald, though the stronger, keeps back his force in concern for Birkin. Energy is channelled, frustration exorcised, 'selfhood' confirmed, despite a society, a way of living, that is always threatening to take it away. As Birkin says when it is all over, such physical closeness 'makes one sane' (p. 351).

Birkin, as we have seen, wants to keep free from social claims and what he perceives as the inherent possessiveness of woman. In order to maintain his precarious independence he seeks to supplement his relationship with Ursula with a different kind of love, the love of a man. Maybe such a love would save Gerald from himself by forcing him into an unorthodox but creative relationship, but he is too bound by convention to accept the challenge. He drifts to his death and Birkin is left with Ursula.

Such an unusual pattern of relationships and needs throws up some awkward questions about the place of role and gender and the nature of identity in 'love', and about what it is we mean when we say that we love. Such questions are disturbing, not at all like the predictable dilemmas of courtship and adultery in the normal 'love' story. The point I wish to make, very firmly, is that there is no possibility of 'tidying up' these questions as readers. The text is 'open', innovative and radical. The debate is continuous, the problems unresolvable. It you are unsympathetic to Lawrence, this is a source of irritation; if you are sympathetic, it is the source of the novel's power.

In conclusion, I want to return to the way the novel is organised as a text. I said earlier that traditional narrative patterns could not encompass Lawrence's extremely pessimistic vision of a society in crisis where individuals can no longer find a meaningful place or moral purpose outside themselves. How can one write a novel when the creative tension between the individual and society no longer operates? Instead characters 'float free' of the constraints of daily living in *Women in Love*, or those that do exist, such as the Brangwen household or Ursula's school, are not fully documented. Lawrence writes a novel that has no past, no future and no plot, save the tenuous development of two love affairs.

I think the chapter headings give us a clue to Lawrence's technique and his method of solving this problem. If you run your eye down the contents page 'Sisters', 'Shortlands', 'Class-Room', 'Diver', 'In the Train', 'Crème de Menthe', 'Totem', and so on – you will see that each chapter is focused on an apparently random encounter, incident, place, occasion or thing. Some of the headings such as 'Continental' and 'Excuse', are rather abstract and so do not set the scene in quite the same way. The chapters vary in their length and elaboration, but they are all structured around a debate, scenes of violent symbolic presentation, or a mixture of both. 'Story-telling' in the old fashioned sense is kept to a minimum.

Such a departure from traditional narrative requires new reading skills. I hope I have demonstrated some of these, implicitly at least, in my own discussion of the novel. We, as readers, have to make connections, see the parallels and contrasts between the chapters and draw our own conclusions. This is what I have done in comparing Birkin and Ursula's first meeting with that of Gerald and Gudrun, and Gerald's domination of the rabbit with his wrestling-bout with Birkin. You might want to go on and compare Birkin and Ursula's night together in Sherwood Forest ('Excuse') with Gerald's invasion of Gudrun's bed in the next chapter ('Death and Love'), or Gudrun, Gerald and the rabbit ('Rabbit') with Birkin, Ursula and the cats ('Mino'), and so on. Compared with the traditional narrative, this novel gives the reader much more responsibility in constructing his or her own meanings, by reading *across* the book – traversing backwards and forwards, comparing and contrasting – as well as *through* it. We do not get a sense of Lawrence dominating and controlling our responses from outside. Events as well as characters are allowed to speak for themselves.

As for the social element, though individuals are extensively foregrounded, the careful choice of situations, whether it be country house, industrial landscape, London flat or Continental hotel, does give us a panoramic sense of a whole society in a state of chronic sickness: indeed, it would not be an exaggeration to say in its death throes. *Women in Love* was first drafted during the First World War. It displays an extraordinary tendency towards extremes and abstraction as Lawrence writes out the violence he senses in society and himself; it is, literally, an 'inhuman' book – it outrages our sense of the normal. The human form and conventional human behaviour almost disappear. Our sense of 'character' in fiction as rounded and coherent disintegrates; individuals are torn apart by psychic forces they cannot control. I am reminded of the description of the African statue in Halliday's flat: 'It was a terrible face, void, peaked, abstracted almost into meaninglessness by the weight of sensation beneath' (p. 133). Like this depiction of a woman in labour, *Women in Love* is also 'a sheer barbaric thing', a remarkable analysis of the destructive tendencies Lawrence perceived within his society as well as a remarkable love story.

6

Lady Chatterley's Lover (1928)

I Constructing an overall analysis

LAWRENCE'S last novel has always had a special place among his works. In the words of a contemporary reviewer, it is 'a famous author's infamous book'. Banned for thirty years and only readily available after the widely publicised trial in 1960, for many it is the only book of Lawrence's that they have read, or at least know about by general repute, while some Lawrence specialists actively dislike it.

None of us go into the reading of a new novel without certain expectations or prejudices, however vaguely formed: with a novel such as *Lady Chatterley's Lover* it is impossible to read 'innocently'. Literary taste and standards of acceptability have changed significantly since Lawrence wrote the novel, and some would say that this is at least partly owing to the trial, which brought about a relaxation of a system of censorship that had scarcely changed since Victorian times. Still, I think any new reader would begin this novel vaguely aware that it had been considered 'shocking', that it was sexually explicit, and that in it Lawrence uses 'four-letter' words. You are bound to have prejudices of a positive or negative nature; it is best to acknowledge them and use them critically as you read. Ask yourself if this book is living up to your expectations, and, if not, why not? Is there anything that is surprising or unexpected? And so on.

I am going to give you my version of the novel's events so that we can begin that process of examination and investigation.

1 *After reading the novel, think about the story and what kind of pattern you can see in the text*

This is my version of events:

Constance Reid is the daughter of a successful society painter. After an unconventional bohemian upbringing abroad, she returns home at the outbreak of the First World War. She meets and marries Clifford Chatterley, son of a baronet and a member of a smart Cambridge set. Clifford goes to war and returns to inherit his father's estate at Wragby Hall in the industrial Midlands. He is, however, paralysed from the waist down and confined to a wheelchair.

Life at Wragby is very quiet and exclusive. Clifford begins to make a reputation as an avant-garde writer of short stories and has intellectual house parties. The strain of this somewhat rarefied atmosphere begins to have its effect on Connie. She has a brief, unsatisfactory affair with a young dramatist, Michaelis, a member of her husband's artistic circle, and finally her health begins to deteriorate. Pressure from her family forces Clifford to hire a nurse, Mrs Bolton, to look after him.

As Clifford becomes more and more dependent on Mrs Bolton as a menial and confidante, so Connie is able to escape from the house more frequently. A wood beyond the park becomes her habitual refuge.

It is during these visits to the wood that she becomes increasingly conscious of her husband's gamekeeper, Oliver Mellors, and finally they become lovers. She subsequently learns the details of his life. Though of humble origin, Mellors is no simple rustic but a disaffected, self-taught intellectual who held a commission during the war. Convalescent and exhausted, he has returned to his cottage in the wood out of despair at modern society and a wish to live alone, avoiding all human contact. He has an estranged wife living nearby. Connie's relationship with Mellors is so transforming that she comes to reject her old way of life and everything her husband represents. Clifford, meanwhile, under the influence of Mrs Bolton, has turned his interest outwards to his mines and is determined to update their technology and improve their productivity. Impotent himself, Clifford has suggested that, should Connie take a lover and provide Wragby with an heir, it would not affect their marriage, which he regards as above the merely physical. Connie decides to leave for a holiday in Venice, not to find a lover but as preparation for the inevitable separation from her husband. While she is away, she discovers that she is pregnant and news reaches her that gossip and scandal have begun at home. Mellors' wife has begun making trouble and allegations, so Clifford dismisses him.

On her return Connie seeks a divorce, citing an old friend, Duncan Forbes, as the father of her child. This is a pretence to expedite Mellors' divorce, but she does tell her husband the truth at a final meeting. He refuses to divorce her. The novel ends tentatively with the lovers in the enforced separation that is necessary for Mellors' freedom, but both look forward in quiet confidence to a future life together, a life apart from this modern world but full and meaningful.

What are my thoughts after reading the novel through and constructing this account? Well, primarily, I suppose, that, unlike the other novels we have looked at, *Lady Chatterley's Lover* is an old-fashioned story told in a clear, straightforward way. The plot is an old one – in fact, one of the oldest in literature: a woman leaves one man for another. In its bourgeois form of an unhappily married woman leaving a stultifying marriage for an uncertain future with a poor but exciting lover, it produced some of the masterpieces of the nineteenth century. You could call this form the novel of adultery. Unlike those earlier fictions, however, this novel seems to have an extremely simple, formal outline – to be quite base and stark, in fact. I miss the sheer profusion of detail, the range and amplitude I have come to expect in a Lawrence novel. I need to pin this down in detailed study, but I sense that this text is much more author directed than usual. Lawrence's voice is much more insistent; characters seem less 'free', in a way, to surprise us: instead they seem directed from outside. There seems to be an impatience, too. The way the scene is set in the opening chapter is sketchy, almost casual. A great deal of information is thrown together, not lovingly elaborated or carefully structured. Then there is the title. Actually it seems quite misleading to me. As my synopsis makes clear, the emphasis is much more on Connie than on Mellors. It is her state of mind, her development, her choices that are chiefly explored. We inhabit her mind more than any other character's and her point of view predominates, though always mediated and directed by Lawrence himself. The men in her life – Clifford, Mellors, Michaelis and Duncan Forbes – represent distinctly separate ways of life, and this places a strain on our ability to see them as 'rounded' or 'real'. The book seems to be in the grip of an idea, with Lawrence anxious to get his point across.

As I have said, these are vague impressions that must be substantiated by detailed work. To examine a character is usually the most straightforward and immediately rewarding way into a novel. It is clear from our discussion that Connie's own development is likely to yield the quickest results as we work towards our basic analysis. (Page references to the novel relate to the Penguin edition, 1961.)

2 *Select a short passage featuring one of the main characters and try to build upon the ideas you have established so far*

> Connie and Clifford had now been nearly two years at Wragby, living their vague life of absorption in Clifford and his work. Their interests had never ceased to flow together over his work.
>
> They talked and wrestled in the throes of composition, and felt as if something were happening, really happening, really in the void.
>
> And thus far it was a life: in the void. For the rest it was non-existence. Wragby was there, the servants . . . but spectral, not really existing. Connie went for walks in the park, and in the woods that joined the park, and enjoyed the solitude and the mystery, kicking the brown leaves of autumn, and picking the primroses of spring. But it was all a dream; or rather it was like the simulacrum of reality. The oak-leaves were to her like oak-leaves seen ruffling in a mirror, she herself was a figure somebody had read about, picking primroses that were only shadows or memories, or words. No substance to her or anything . . . no touch, no contact! Only this life with Clifford, this endless spinning of webs of yarn, of the minutiae of consciousness, these stories Sir Malcolm said there was nothing in, and they wouldn't last. Why should there be anything in them, why should they last? Sufficient unto the day is the evil thereof. Sufficient unto the moment is the *appearance* of reality. (pp. 19–20)

What's happening here? Lawrence, in his privileged position of author and narrator, is sketching out a process of disillusionment. Partly objectively and partly subjectively as he moves into Connie's consciousness, he reveals her growing awareness of a dissatisfaction with her way of life, her unease at its emptiness and lack of substance. There is a complex tension, skilfully expressed, in Connie's predicament; on the one hand we perceive the lack of reality in her mode of existence, a vacuum of 'void' needing to be filled; on the other, we enter her consciousness and experience her life as a dream, an unawakened trance-like state that registers dissatisfaction but is fearful of change.

If we look at the language of the first paragraph, we can see that expressions of endeavour and commitment are being ironically undercut. Clifford and Connie's self-absorbed life is 'vague'. The ceaseless activity and collaborative effort over Clifford's writing, the 'throes' of composition, only make it *feel* 'as if something were happening'. There is desperation in the repetition of 'really', and the true situation, as Lawrence sees it, is brought home by the finality of 'void'.

The second paragraph takes up and elaborates the idea of Connie living in a void and expresses its nature. Connie is a ghost 'not really existing' in a life surrounded by other ghosts. The cycle of nature is reduced to a second-hand dream, a 'simulacrum' of reality. In her walks oak-leaves are only a reflection and primroses reduced to second-order approximations, 'shadows', 'memories' or 'words'. Even Connie herself is caught up in a fiction not of her own making, and the reference to Clifford's stories that her father rejects as worthless is significant. By living with Clifford, she is caught up, captured, in a web of words, his words. It is a thought-dominated world without real meaning; there is 'no touch, no contact'.

This passage is taken from chapter 2, which describes life at Wragby; it outlines a problem for Connie which will grow ever more critical as the novel progresses. It provides a contact for her first and unsuccessful attempt (in chapter 3) to find touch and contact with a lover. The low-key laconic style that Lawrence adopts here seems casual, but closer examination shows otherwise. Despite the intimate mode of direct address to the reader and the colloquial tone, the narrator is artfully in control. The sentences are simply constructed and loosely strung together, but the reader's attention is held and concentrated by the occasional exact and complexly Latinate phrase – 'simulacrum of reality', 'minutiae of consciousness'. There is also the casual and ironic usage of the biblical phrase with which the second paragraph concludes: it is used flippantly but then repeated, suitably and subtly adapted, to make a more serious authorial comment on Connie's false situation and false consciousness.

We have examined Connie's state of mind at the beginning of the novel's action. Now I should like to look at a passage that gives us some sense of her relationship with her husband.

3 *Select a second passage for discussion*

> 'I'm sorry we can't have a son,' she said.
>
> He looked at her steadily, with his full, pale-blue eyes.
>
> 'It would almost be a good thing if you had a child by another man,' he said. 'If we brought it up at Wragby, it would belong to us and to the place. I don't believe very intensely in fatherhood. If we had the child to rear, it would be our own, and it would carry on. Don't you think it's worth considering?'
>
> Connie looked up at him at last. The child, her child, was just an 'it' to him. It . . . it . . . it!
>
> 'But what about the other man?' she asked.
>
> 'Does it matter very much? Do these things really affect us very deeply? . . . You had that lover in Germany . . . what is it now? Nothing almost. It seems to me that it isn't these little acts and little connexions we make in our lives that matter so very much. They pass away, and where are they? Where . . . where are the snows of yesteryear? . . . It's what endures through one's life that matters; my own life matters to me, in its long continuance and development. But what do the occasional connexions matter? And the occasional sexual connexions especially! If people don't exaggerate them ridiculously, they pass like the mating of birds. And so they should. What does it matter? It's the life-long companionship that matters. It's the living together from day to day, not the sleeping together once or twice. You and I are married, no matter what happens to us. We have the habit of each other. And habit, to my thinking, is more vital than any occasional excitement. The long, slow, enduring thing . . . that's what we live by . . . not the occasional spasm of any sort. Little by little, living together, two people fall into a sort of unison, they vibrate so intricately to one another. That's the real secret of marriage, not sex; at least not the simple function of sex. You and I are interwoven in a marriage. If we stick to that we ought to be able to arrange this sex thing, as we arrange going to the dentist; since fate has given us a checkmate physically there!'
>
> Connie sat and listened in a sort of wonder, and a sort of fear. She did not know if he was right or not. (pp. 46–7)

This is part of an episode in chapter 5 where Clifford, in one of their visits to the wood, suggests that Connie might have a child by another man to maintain the Chatterley inheritance at Wragby. He insists that the sexual intimacy necessary would not make him jealous because their marriage exists on a higher plane. Connie remains unconvinced and rather disturbed. There is a tension between the bland reasonableness of his proposal and her confused, emotional response.

It is understandable that Connie should waver, because there is no doubt that Clifford is good with words. He is persuasive and, superficially at least, there is a lot of sense in what he says. It is difficult not to assent to the sentiments expressed in such phrases as 'the slow, enduring thing . . . that is what we live by' or 'it's the life-long companionship that matters. It's the living together from day to day, not the sleeping together once or twice.' Clifford has a real point, we feel, when he states that the basis of marriage lies in close habituation rather than the vicissitudes of sexual desire. And the sentiments are so civilised and so eloquently expressed. 'Where are the snows of yesteryear?' is a quotation from Dante Gabriel Rossetti, the Victorian poet; Clifford has a well-stocked mind and is never at a loss for the apt literary reference.

It is only when we see these remarks in their full context that Clifford's inhumanity and frozen incapacity for feeling becomes apparent. A child for Clifford is an 'it', a possession to be owned by a place. It is to be 'Wragby's child', not part of an intimate family bond – 'I don't believe very intensely in fatherhood' – but an inheritor. Breeding for Clifford is a matter of class, possessions and inheritance. It is habit rather than true intimacy that Clifford favours, and to call habit 'vital' is a particular piece of semantic nonsense that shows Clifford does not always respect the words he uses with such facility. It is natural, of course, for Clifford to underplay what he cannot do, but his distaste and denigration of sexuality implies an endemic dislike of which his paralysis, what he punningly calls his 'checkmate', is merely the outward sign and confirmation.

At this point in the novel Connie is implicated in Clifford's view of sex as something mechanical, devoid of emotion and loyalty, 'a simple function' to be arranged 'like going to the dentist'. Her human lovers and her affair with Michaelis are relationships based on 'this sex thing'; they can be easily dismissed as 'little acts and little connexions', 'occasional excitements' or 'spasms'. Such a view, of course, reduces our humanity; it lowers our sexual relationships beneath the 'mating of birds'. It represents an abuse of our powers and capacities, a blasphemy on life. Connie realises this intuitively but is powerless to resist his specious reasoning until life teaches her differently. She is still in a state of atrophied feeling. Compromised by her affair with Michaelis, which is exactly the kind of relationship that Clifford assumes all sexual feeling to be, she is bound theoretically to acquiesce, even though her deeper feelings tell her that Clifford's logic is all wrong. This discussion ends with her first meeting with Mellors, who is going to end all this mental unreality.

Finally, what does this passage tell us about Connie's relationship to Clifford? I think it shows Clifford's need to dominate, even bully, Connie intellectually. It is the relationship of tutor to pupil. It is also a good example of how Connie is caught up a web of words and is instinctively struggling to escape. Lawrence gives her a passive, listening role here, the better to allow Clifford to condemn himself out of his own mouth, but there is enough in her response to suggest her powers of resistance and a capacity for change.

It would make sense to move on now and see the kind of relationship Connie has with Mellors and what feelings he evokes in her.

4 *Select a third passage for discussion*

> So she went round the side of the house. At the back of the cottage the land rose steeply, so the back yard was sunken, and enclosed by a low stone wall. She turned the corner of the house and stopped. In the little yard two paces beyond her, the man was washing himself, utterly unaware. He was naked to the hips, his velveteen breeches slipping down over his slender loins. And his white slim back was curved over a big bowl of soapy water, in which he ducked his head, shaking his head with a queer, quick little motion, lifting his slender white arms, and pressing the soapy water from his ears, quick, subtle as a weasel playing with water, and utterly alone. Connie backed away round the corner of the house, and hurried away to the wood. In spite of herself, she had had a shock. After all, merely a man washing himself; commonplace enough, Heaven knows!
>
> Yet in some curious way it was a visionary experience: it had hit her in the middle of the body. She saw the clumsy breeches slipping down over the pure, delicate, white loins, the bones showing a little, and the sense of aloneness, of a creature purely alone, overwhelmed her. Perfect, white, solitary nudity of a creature that lives alone, and inwardly alone. And beyond that, a certain beauty of a pure creature. Not the stuff of beauty, not even the body of beauty, but a lambency, the warm, white flame of a single life, revealing itself in contours that one might touch: a body!
>
> Connie had received the shock of vision in her womb, and she knew it; it lay inside her. But with her mind she was inclined to ridicule. A man washing himself in a backyard! No doubt with evil-smelling yellow soap! She was rather annoyed; why should she be made to stumble on these vulgar privacies? (pp. 69–70)

This encounter takes place in chapter 6, when Connie has yet to speak to the gamekeeper. She visits him in his cottage to give him a message from Clifford and sees him washing himself outside, unaware of her presence. As readers we experience the encounter from Connie's point of view and, superficially, it seems ordinary enough, but Lawrence chooses to emphasise its visionary and revelatory qualities. There is this disparity between a commonplace experience, potentially embarrassing though it might be, and its disturbing effect on Connie, which seems to go beyond all reason.

It is part of Lawrence's skill as a writer that he can re-create and make his readers 'live through' an experience as they read, however humble and ordinary it might be. Here, with and through Connie, we experience the essential mystery of identity, the 'otherness' of another person. Connie is surprised into the extraordinary uniqueness of the experience before class and social prejudices seek to diminish and resist it. We can see both processes taking place in the passage, a kind of 'take' as Connie sees the man and a 'double-take' as she wanders away reliving the experience, trying to make sense of it and finally seeking to reduce it to proportion in her mind.

The first paragraph concentrates on the man and his movements. He is very much in motion, curving his back, lifting his arms, ducking and shaking his head 'with queer, quick little actions'. He reveals himself in his movements, alive like a flame, warm and ever-changing. Lawrence is at pains to show us the 'contours that one might touch': the way the loins, slender and white, bones showing, are defined by the loose breeches, and the 'slender white arms' raised to press water from the ears after the back has been bent over the bowl. Mellors in his unselfconscious solitude is seen in the context of the natural world; he is a 'creature', a duck bobbing up from the water or 'subtle as a weasel'.

The second paragraph reveals the effect on Connie. She has been startled into an apprehension of the physical, the splendour and distinctive individuality of a human body, quite beautiful in its absorbed solitude and self-sufficiency. The effect on her is also physical; she feels it in her 'womb', in the middle of her body.

In the third paragraph Connie shows herself to be split in her consciousness. Her body reacts intuitively to the experience, but her mind rebels, seeks to reassert its control. Typically it does this through social prejudices: the man is working-class so his actions are 'vulgar'; he is washing himself with cheap yellow soap in a 'backyard'. What could be so significant about that?

I think the first two passages and a comparison between Lawrence's description of Clifford and his description here of Mellors will give us an answer to that. We know Clifford by his speech – indeed, most of the time he is presented as a 'talking head'. I am sure you can find for yourself passages that support this view. Talk is his distinguishing feature and he is presented through his language, in particular his passion for gossip, intellectual discussion and abstract debate. He is always conscious of his social status and always placed in a social context. As I think the first passage shows, Clifford's world is a mental world; it is a remote, second-hand world that Connie, starved of contact and touch, is desperate to escape. Mellors in contrast is physically presented here celebrating the body – his unique body – in silence and in an unself-conscious manner that transcends categories and labels. Washing is just one of many domestic tasks we see him perform in the book, along with making fires, mending coops, handling chicks, preparing meals. Above all it is important that we see him alone in nature. He lives in the wood with other living things, free from the social forces that have shaped, and snared, Clifford and his friends. It is in this natural context that Mellors can lead Comnie into her realisation of the body and the possibility of touch.

Let us now examine a passage about Connie and Mellors after they have become lovers, in order to assess his effect on her.

5 *Select a fourth passage for discussion*

> 'Are you sure you've not hurt yourself?' she said fiercely.
>
> He shook his head. She looked at his smallish, short, alive hand, browned by the weather. It was the hand that caressed her. She had never even looked at it before. It seemed so still, like him, with a curious inward stillness that made her want to clutch it, as if she could not reach it. All her soul suddenly swept towards him: he was so silent, and out of reach! And he felt his limbs revive. Shoving with his left hand, he laid his right on her round white wrist, softly enfolding her wrist, with a caress. And the flame of strength went down his back and his loins, reviving him. And she bent suddenly and kissed his hand. Meanwhile the back of Clifford's head was held sleek and motionless, just in front of them.
>
> At the top of the hill they rested, and Connie was glad to let

> go. She had had fugitive dreams of friendship between these two men: one her husband, the other the father of her child. Now she saw the screaming absurdity of her dreams. The two males were as hostile as fire and water. They mutually exterminated one another. And she realized for the first time what a queer subtle thing hate is. For the first time, she had consciously and definitely hated Clifford, with vivid hate: as if he ought to be obliterated from the face of the earth. And it was strange, how free and full of life it made her feel, to hate him and to admit it fully to herself. – 'Now I've hated him, I shall never be able to go on living with him', came the thought into her mind. (pp. 199–200)

Here Connie is assisting Mellors in his efforts to push Clifford's broken mechanical wheelchair out of the wood. The episode is very important, because it brings Connie to her moment of choice between the two men in her concern for the gamekeeper's exhaustion. The tension lies within Connie herself, between her care and concern for Mellors and her hatred of her husband. She realises that they stand for quite different systems of value and opposing ways of life. Compromise is impossible. The significance of the moment is heightened by the close proximity of all three of them.

If we contrast Connie's character here with the description of her walking in the wood in our first passage, I think we can see quite a change in Lawrence's treatment of her. Before she was depicted as a somnambulist, walking through the park in a trance-like state of unreality. There is no doubt that Connie is now alive. This is no 'simulacrum of reality'; she is awake and in touch with her feelings. The hand she wants to touch, brown and still, is alive and has 'brought her to life'. It is the only part of Mellors we see here, but it arrests and focuses her concern by its unique particularity; in contrast, the 'sleek and motionless' head of the impervious Clifford is like that of a tailor's dummy. The whole of the first paragraph is a demonstration of the power of touch and its restorative effects. The communication between the pair is also intuitive and non-verbal. Her need to touch him, his awareness of her concern and his response all take place in silence. Clifford's pontifications about love are no substitute, we feel, for this silent demonstration and emblem of it, a wrist clasped and a hand kissed. The sense of intimate mutuality is reinforced by the mobility of viewpoint. As we read we seem to be both outside, observing, and inside, experiencing the action. We also move dynamically with the flow of emotion from one to the other and back again. In external action, internal emotion, and the relationship between them, the emphasis is always on flow and reciprocity. Connie wants to 'clutch' his hand; her soul 'sweeps' towards him. Mellors 'revives'; he 'softly enfolds' her wrist and feels strength run down his back and loins. It is in this ability to make us, the readers, experience and empathise with such private emotions that the power of the passage lies. It is one of Lawrence's particular gifts.

The second paragraph concerns Connie's examination of herself and her feelings as a consequence of her love for Mellors. Clearly there is no attempt to be fair or objective, no room for compromise. The mutual antagonism of the two men is total and elemental, like fire and water. Connie's hope of compromise is exposed as fantasy. She sees the impossibility of splitting the role of husband from that of father of her child, a split that Clifford earlier had argued was possible – and nearly convinced her about. Her feelings for Clifford have a new realism and honesty that you might find shocking. There is no attempt to be 'fair' to Clifford, no room for pity. Hate is seen as a 'pure', liberating emotion not to be repressed or guiltily rejected. It gives Connie access to life. This could be viewed as refreshingly unsentimental, an indication of how energised and determined Connie has now become; or it could be considered brutal. In some ways this is a brutal book – after all, a wife here wishes her crippled husband dead – and we must not shirk the implications of this when we move on to consider other aspects of it. We have to consider whether the treatment of Clifford and Lawrence's manifest hostility to him and everything he stands for weakens the book or contributes to its strength; whether the unorthodox black-and-white morality he displays in such passages as this works with or against the vivid re-creation of 'felt life' that is such a feature of Lawrence's best writing. We shall all of us, I suspect, come to different conclusions about this according to temperament. It is one of the issues – perhaps the most important one – that divides the novel's critics.

Let us now take a short passage from the end of the novel to get a sense of Connie's full development.

6 *Select a fifth passage for discussion*

> She took off her things, and made him do the same. She was lovely in the soft first flush of her pregnancy.

> 'I ought to leave you alone,' he said.
>
> 'No!' she said. 'Love me! Love me, and say you'll keep me. Say you'll keep me! Say you'll never let me go, to the world nor to anybody.'
>
> She crept close against him, clinging fast to his thin, strong naked body, the only home she had ever known.
>
> 'Then I'll keep thee,' he said. 'If tha wants it, then I'll keep thee.'
>
> He held her round and fast.
>
> 'And say you're glad about the child,' she repeated. 'Kiss it! Kiss my womb and say you're glad it's there.'
>
> But that was more difficult for him.
>
> 'I've a dread of putting' children i' th' world,' he said. 'I've such a dread o' th' future for 'em.'
>
> 'But you've put it into me. Be tender to it, and that will be its future already. Kiss it!'
>
> He quivered, because it was true. 'Be tender to it, and that will be its future.' – At that moment he felt a sheer love for the woman. He kissed her belly and her mound of Venus, to kiss close to the womb and the foetus with the womb.
>
> 'Oh, you love me! You love me!' she said, in a little cry like one of her blind, inarticulate love cries. And he went in to her softly, feeling the stream of tenderness flowing in release from his bowels to hers, the bowels of compassion kindled between them. (pp. 289–90)

This episode occurs on Connie's return from Venice pregnant with Mellors' child. She sees him again in London and convinces him that they can have a future together. We can see that the tension resolved in this scene is between Mellors' uncertainty, his fear of life's demands and responsibilities, and Connie's courage, her commitment to the future exemplified in her unborn child.

I suppose a lazy version of the novel's events given to someone who had not read it would give the impression that *Lady Chatterley's Lover* is a story of passion triumphing over class when the potency of a working man proves irresistible to a well-born lady. There is some truth in this, but also much that is misleading. It makes the book sound like a fiction about seduction that falls into the clichés of pornography or romantic love, or a mixture of the two. A passage such as the one just quoted draws attention to the much more complex, and original, nature of the writing. There is no question here of a hapless, passive heroine caught up in her passion for a strong, dominant male intent on his own pleasure, though, to be fair, there are other episodes that do conform more to this paradigm. What a careful reading will show, I think, is that human loving and human needing between two people is a very complex business involving a wide range of emotions on both sides. There are thirteen 'episodes of sexual intercourse', as the prosecution counsel put it in the 1960 trial; but to go on and assert, as he did, that the only variation between them is the time and place is grotesque and perverse misreading. I think you will find each is different and each part of an evolving pattern. In this, the last, it is Connie who is the stronger. She is the one prepared to take initiatives, to be brave and hopeful. It is Mellors who is weak and vulnerable. If we had any doubts after the previous passage, this one dispels any notions of him as a bold, simple-minded rustic.

Much of the passage is in dialogue and most of this takes the form of urgent, simple imperatives or statements. The language is pared right down to essentials, yet it is markedly repetitive: 'love, 'say' and 'kiss' are repeated five times, 'keep' four times, 'glad', 'womb', 'bowels', 'tender', and 'dread' twice, all in a short extract. In addition whole phrases and syntactical constructions recur: 'Then I'll keep thee', 'say you're glad', 'I've a dread', 'Be tender to it', 'you love me', 'say you'll keep me', 'Kiss it!' are all repeated, or reproduced with small variations. Sometimes orders are reproduced as answering statements or actions. For example: 'Say you'll keep me!'/'Then I keep thee', and 'Kiss my womb'/'He kissed her belly.' In other words, there is a very high degree of formal patterning in the language, and this stresses the mutual dependency that exists between the lovers. If there is a tension or difference in the language, it is between Connie's use of standard English and Mellors' use of dialect, it is a difference of class that is registered but healed, resolved in physical tenderness. Speech finally becomes akin to 'blind, inarticulate love cries'; language gives way to touch, the kiss that is both a gesture of acceptance and a symbol of benediction on the unborn child. It is touch that Mellors says a page earlier is 'our crying need'.

'He went into her softly' is a description of the sexual act that is direct and unevasive, but this is followed by a complicated, metaphorical exploration of the experience from Mellors' point of view. As so often before, Lawrence takes risks in an attempt to express the inexpressible. To write of 'the stream of tenderness flowing in release from his bowels to hers' is, of course, to risk laughter, and the risk is compounded by talk of bowels 'kindled between them'. It is nonsense, but a nonsense that states a kind of truth. 'Bowels' is an Old Testament usage, and by employing it here, along with 'womb' and 'belly', Lawrence attempts to place the centre of feeling in the physical, as far away as possible from mental control and mental self-consciousness. But Lawrence doesn't exhort sheer mindlessness: 'foetus', after all, is a very precise medical term.

Overall, I would say that the tone of the passage is defiant: 'the only home' that the lovers have is each other; it is the tenderness of two against the world. Touch and tenderness are the embattled centres of resistance against the evils of what Lawrence sees as an over-mental world, too preoccupied with material things. Such a passage is part of the bedrock of Lawrence's metaphysic in this novel.

7 *Have I achieved a sufficiently complex sense of the novel?*

We could, of course, go on and cover more episodes and so build up a more complete sense of Connie's relationships with Clifford and Mellors, but I think we have done enough to get a sense of the book's orientation and pattern. It should be clear that *Lady Chatterley's Lover* is more than just a love story. Connie is our representative caught between two ways of life and living. We, the readers, live and experience in close relationship with the heroine and so are asked to approve and vindicate her choice. The two opposing ways of life are summarised in the attitudes, behaviour and way of life of Clifford and Mellors. Clifford leads a mental life at the expense of a physical one, for him, words are a substitute for living. He inhabits a social world which is seen as alienating, insensitive, class-conscious and manipulative. The consequences of this way of life are deadly if its effects are truthfully rendered in Connie's deteriorating health. Mellors, on the other hand, strives for harmony between the mental and physical life, and a vital interaction between words and deeds. He seeks true individuality, and this is best achieved when man places himself in the context of the natural world outside society. Though this may mean a more solitary existence, we are asked to believe that such an existence is more authentic and more fully human. When Connie chooses Mellors she is choosing life itself. There is no room for compromise and, what is more, no room for complication. There is no doubt in the novelist's mind how she, and by implication we, must choose. You might find this bullying and oppressive. Certainly this book is not giving us the openness and provisionality, the sense of many options, that we have come to expect from 'realistic' novels. Is it diminished because of this? After all, what kind of novel is it?

This, and other problems, we can now move on to consider. Of course, I shall not be able to cover them all. High on my list of priorities is more work on Mellors. He seems to stand for too many things, and is used to give vent to too many grievances. Also I feel we should look at the sexual explicitness, particularly in the use of taboo-breaking language, and ask ourselves what was Lawrence's intention and whether he was successful in realising it. There is the symbolic patterning of the novel to consider. Is it too obtrusive? Finally, I think we need to ask ourselves how the lives of the characters are contextualised in the wider world of events and consequences. We are all caught up in the flow of history – and we can't all live in woods.

II Aspects of the novel

One of the ways in which Mrs Bolton diverts Clifford Chatterley after her arrival at Wragby is to 'talk Tevershall' or gossip to him about local affairs. Lawrence goes on, 'It was more than gossip. It was Mrs Gaskell and George Eliot and Miss Mitford all rolled into one.' Clifford is intrigued; in fact Mrs Bolton becomes his window on the world beyond the gates of Wragby Hall. He gets information for his stories from her and it is through her influence that he takes a fresh interest in his mines. Connie's response is rather more ambiguous:

> Connie was fascinated, listening to her. But afterwards always a little ashamed. She ought not to listen with this queer rabid curiosity. After all, one may hear the most private affairs of other people, but only in a spirit of respect for the struggling, battered thing which any human soul is, and in a spirit of fine, discriminative sympathy. For even satire is a form of sympathy. It is the way our sympathy flows and recoils that really determines our lives. And here lies the vast importance of the novel, properly handled. It can inform and lead into new places the flow of our sympathetic consciousness, and it can lead our sympathy away in recoil from things gone dead. Therefore, the novel, properly handled, can reveal the most secret places of life: for it is in the *passional* secret places of life, above all, that the tide of sensitive awareness needs to ebb and flow, cleansing and freshening.

> But the novel, like gossip, can also excite spurious sympathies and recoils, mechanical and deadening to the psyche. The novel can glorify the most corrupt feelings, so long as they are *conventionally* 'pure'. Then the novel, like gossip, becomes at last vicious, and, like gossip, all the more vicious, because it is always ostensibly on the side of the angels. (p. 105)

Now, although this passage begins as Connie's response, it is clear that after the first two sentences the comments and criticism are Lawrence's own. There is nothing new in such direct interventions. They are common in nineteenth-century novels, but unusual in sophisticated modern fiction. It is a measure of Lawrence's earnestness and concern to get his views across that he is prepared to speak directly to us in this way. In this piece of unadorned literary criticism he defends his view of what a novel should be and do as distinct from the conventional novel of 'gossip'. In attacking the novel of 'gossip', Lawrence is rejecting a whole tradition of regional, provincial novel writing from Jane Austen to George Eliot. He is rejecting what he sees as its outmoded literary procedures and the conventional morality that underpins them. They are 'things gone dead', with inappropriate concerns and techniques for the truly modern novelist and the serious issues that he, or she, must address. To avoid being 'mechanical' and 'deadening', novelists must avoid the stereotypical judgements of gossip; instead they must explore new areas of life and living, and force us, the readers, to confront and acknowledge them. By doing this, the novelist can 'cleanse' us like the sea, and force us to redefine our lives and our priorities for living in a way no other artist can.

My paraphrase does not do justice to the splendour or the persuasiveness of the writing, but the whole passage is a useful clue to Lawrence's intentions in writing *Lady Chatterley's Lover* and the ways in which it differs from other, more conventional fictions. It alerts us to Lawrence's strenuous moral concern, however eccentric or unorthodox we may feel this to be, and why he is prepared to take the risks he does to get his message across. So what distinguishes *Lady Chatterley's Lover* from the novel of 'gossip'? I said at the beginning that it was in the grip of an idea, and our efforts in the first half of this chapter were directed at finding out what this might be. I think we have already obtained a sense of how Lawrence bends and distorts characters and situations to further his views; of how he directs the flow of our sympathies towards Connie and Mellors and away, in recoil, from the 'deadness' of Clifford and everything he stands for. The least of Lawrence's concerns in this text is to be 'fair' in any conventional sense. Of course, characters are never 'free' in novels, but Lawrence doesn't even bother to provide the illusion of autonomy. Instead he uses characters to demonstrate or articulate ideas, often in ways that strain our notions of the probable. In this sense, *Lady Chatterley's Lover* is a fiction but not properly a novel in the accepted sense. At many points Lawrence disappoints our expectations that characters should be 'rounded', their actions plausible and their environments accurately described. He rejects these expectations as inadequate, along with the conventions by which they are inscribed in a text; they are simply not up to the urgency of his message. Of course, you can reject the message along with the techniques that Lawrence uses but it is as well to understand Lawrence's intention before you dismiss *Lady Chatterley's Lover* as a poor, because 'unrealistic', novel.

One way of dealing with this problem of the novel's 'truth to life' is to see it, at least in part, as Lawrence's attempt to write a moral fable: that is, a fiction with clear didactic intentions using a rather rigid and biased form of narrative to impose them on the reader. Of course, all novels set out to persuade us to a point of view, but *Lady Chatterley's Lover* is more transparent in this respect. If you dislike the message, it is easy to dismiss the text as crude; if you are more favourably disposed, you might find Lawrence refreshingly direct and honest.

We can set out to teach in two ways: we can either discuss or demonstrate, and I think it is easy to see how the text falls into this basic pattern. There is a great deal of talk in the book. Clifford, as we have seen, likes the sound of his own voice, but so does nearly everyone else. Lawrence sets up the terms of his debate in the intellectual house-party discussions early in the novel. Characters such as Hammond, May and Tommy Dukes voice their opinions about personal relationships and the malaise of modern life, then simply fade out of the story. No attempt is made to give them fictional substance. They are there, quite simply, to rehearse arguments. At first it seems that the book is going to revolve around a contrast between empty, abstract talk and emotionally charged physical contact and healing silence. Connie grows tired of words and drifts towards the wood's 'potency of silence'. The courtship and initial lovemaking of

Connie and Mellors is mostly conducted in silence; it's all the more powerful and effective for that.

However, this is not a contrast that Lawrence is able to sustain. I expect you were as surprised as I was when, midway through the love, Mellors, the taciturn dialect-speaker, suddenly turned disaffected intellectual. Thereafter he is very voluble and presents an uneasy mixture of registers and language styles. To this extent he becomes a far less credible figure than Clifford. Not all the time, but for a significant part of it, he seems to lose psychological plausibility and becomes a mouthpiece for Lawrence's doctrinaire polemic. Clifford does at least have the awful and developing consistency of a grotesque or cartoon figure. Let me try to illustrate what I mean.

> The man looked down in silence at the tense phallus, that did not change. – 'Ay!' he said at last, in a little voice. 'Ay ma lad! tha're theer right enough. Yi, tha mun rear thy head! Theer on thy own, eh? An' ta'es no count o' nob'dy! Tha ma'es nowt o' me, John Thomas. Art boss? Of me? Eh well, tha're more cocky than me, an' tha says less. John Thomas! Dost want *her*? Dost want may lady Jane? Tha's dipped me in again, tha hast. Ay, an'tha comes up smilin'. – Ax'er then! Ax lady Jane! Say: Lift up your heads o' ye Gates, that the King of Glory may come in. Ay, th' cheek on thee! Cunt, that's what tha're after. Tell lady Jane tha wants cunt. John Thomas, an' th' cunt o' lady Jane!' (p. 218)

I suppose my first response to this is to think how abstract and artificial it is, particularly in the context of passionate love-making. Lawrence has not only taken us into the 'passional, secret-places' avoided by most novelists but has stopped and used Mellors to preach to us there. This kind of reflexive commentary on his own sexuality is either comic or makes Mellors even more inhuman that Clifford. With much less excuse he is substituting words for deeds. Such scenes are a world away from those marvellously rendered and touchingly eloquent moments of first contact where two people in need reach out dumbly for each other. As we have seen before, Lawrence is very bold in his efforts to take language into taboo areas of human experience and the human psyche. In a discussion of this book, he writes of the modern need to express 'the full conscious realization of sex'. In this instance, and others like it, you may feel that he fails in his own declared aim of bringing a sensitive awareness that 'cleanses and freshens' to these secret places.

Part of the difficulty is that he has to sacrifice certain conventions of expression and behaviour that support our sense of the acceptably real or likely. For example, words do accrue their meanings in social contexts; we cannot individually reinvent them, however much we might wish to. In trying to use such a word as 'cunt' in tender, even meditative contexts, Lawrence is working against the grain of the language in a provocative, self-defeating way. Its negative associations are just too strong, On the other hand, you might feel that one has to start somewhere if one wants to effect change and revolutionise feelings. Lawrence has at least initiated a process whereby a brutal swear-word might be retrieved into a more loving and tender context. It is a very delicate and complex issue, one you need to have thought through to your own satisfaction if you are studying this book seriously. One thing is clear: you can't fault Lawrence for courage.

On a more general level, this passage exactly illustrates that uneasy mixture of language styles that becomes a feature of Lawrence's presentation of Mellors. The dialect is there to show the intimate context, and that Mellors is speaking directly and honestly as a working man. But the content, as I have said, is really rather abstract and theoretical. One can see what Lawrence is trying to do. He wants to get across his sense of the essentially impersonal nature of desire as it possesses and then leaves each individual, but it is difficult to see as anything but bizarre, in ways that I am doubtful Lawrence intended, his device of having Mellors conduct an imaginary dialogue with his own personified erect member in order to educate his partner into the phallic mysteries. The resulting uncertainty of tone makes it difficult for us to know how to respond. In any conventional sense, this is 'unrealistic' writing depicting an 'unrealistic' situation. And this is further compounded when a blunt working man suddenly breaks into an adaptation of Psalm 24. Again, there are two ways to respond to such episodes. The first is to say that Lawrence the theoriser and preacher has set himself too hard a task and that his skills as a novelist desert him. The second is to admit all that, but to go on and add that it is just this unevenness – the way that Lawrence breaks through the constraints of the orthodox novel – that gives the book its curious power to evoke strong responses from its readers.

When using that other teaching aid, namely demonstration,

Lawrence displays a much surer touch. The early love scenes between Connie and Mellors are sympathetically rendered, and, when Lawrence is content to 'show' rather than 'tell', the power of his argument is self-evident. He is able to draw upon his undoubted abilities with those traditional novelist's skills of narrative, power of description and psychological insight. As I have said, in some ways *Lady Chatterley's Lover* is a traditional story told in an old-fashioned way. True, there is distortion, particularly in the development of Clifford's character, but this does seem to have a kind of grisly consistency in its own terms, rather like a cruel comic strip. As Lawrence wrote 'satire is a kind of sympathy', and, charged with his hatred, Clifford playing with his wireless, improving his mines, reading Racine, or in his perverse relationship with Mrs Bolton, had a kind of coherence that Mellors never quite achieves.

Let us look again at chapter 13. Clifford, you remember, invades the peaceful wood in his noisy, mechanical chair and gives Connie a lecture on the necessity of an industrial society based on class hostility and the reduction of workers to functions within a vast social machine. The wasteful brutality of such philosophy of life is then demonstrated by Clifford's wheelchair as it leaves a trail of destruction in its wake and finally breaks down. Clifford is reduced to impotent rage and has to be extricated from his own mess by Connie and Mellors at some cost to themselves. Here, it seems to me, discussion and demonstration mesh together convincingly. The symbolism of the chair, its destructiveness and limitations, is self-evident but works well in the broad, satirical context that accompanies Clifford where ever he goes.

Now let us return to the last passage I quoted. There discussion and demonstration do not work together nearly so well. There is something quirky and eccentric in the spectacle of a man addressing his own penis. We recognise that Lawrence is trying to make a symbolic point, but the symbolism works against our sense of the plausible and likely rather than with it. Part of the problem is that Clifford, however stylised, is a recognisable product of a class: he has a class voice and a class point of view. Mellors is miraculously free of such determinants, and this is indicated by his bewildering changes of role and language – at one moment an anguished intellectual, at the next an earthy primitive taking Connie out of class and time. They become 'John Thomas' and 'Lady Jane'. This move of the characters into a kind of mythical dimension is further developed in the following chapter, where they run naked in the wood and adorn their bodies with wild flowers.

Now, the novel as a form has evolved with 'gossip' very much in mind. In other words, it is a kind of fiction that does deal with characters that are determined by class values, who are subject to social discipline, and have to work out the consequences of their actions in time. Such scenes as these create difficulties for the reader because Lawrence is uncertain about his own method. In part he does want to satisfy our expectations, but it is also true that he wishes to challenge and disrupt them. He is out to shake our complacency and work for radical change. It is up to each of us to decide whether this clash or dissonance of method is self-defeating or stimulating and interesting despite the obvious difficulties. I think that Lawrence seeks to resolve his own inconsistencies by organising his text around powerful, well-established patterns of symbolism and myth. It is these that I should now like to explore.

We have seen from our basic analysis that *Lady Chatterley's Lover* is a very structured book. The text is built around an antithesis or clash of contrasting ideas that are expressed not only by the characters of Clifford and Mellors but also by the contrasting landscapes that they inhabit. Here is a description of one of them:

> The car ploughed uphill through the long squalid straggle of Tevershall, the blackened brick dwellings, the black slate roofs glistening their sharp edges, the mud black with coal-dust, the pavements wet and black. It was as if dismalness had soaked through and through everything. The utter negation of natural beauty, the utter negation of the gladness of life, the utter absence of the instinct for shapely beauty which every bird and beast has, the utter death of the human intuitive faculty was appalling. The stacks of soap in the grocers' shops, the rhubarb and lemons in the greengrocers! the awful hats in the milliners! all went by ugly, ugly, ugly, followed by the plaster-and-gilt horror of the cinema with its wet picture announcements, 'A Woman's Love!', and the new big Primitive chapel, primitive enough in its stark brick and big panes of greenish and raspberry glass in the windows. The Wesleyan chapel, higher up, was of blackened brick and stood behind iron railings and blackened shrubs. The Congregational chapel, which thought itself superior, was built of rusticated sandstone and had a steeple, but not a very high one. Just beyond were the new school buildings, expensive pink brick, and gravelled playground inside iron railings,

> all very imposing, and mixing the suggestion of a chapel and a prison. (p. 158)

Tevershall is Clifford's kingdom: it is dominated by him socially as master of Wragby Hall, and it is created by him industrially as owner of the pits that provide the work and wealth that make the environment. Though we see nominally through Connie's eyes, it is Lawrence, his voice, his vision, that predominates. There is no more attempt to be 'fair' here than there is in the presentation of Clifford's character. All the most formidable resources of Lawrence's rhetoric are mobilised to present the most negative vision possible of the consequences of industrialisation. In such passages we move away from the personal into a wholesale social critique. Tevershall is seen as something ugly and something dead, mechanical and imprisoning. The crude uniformity is emphasised by the repetition of 'utter' and 'ugly', the pun on 'primitive', and the way that institutional buildings are surrounded by iron railings. There is a deliberate selection of only the most dreary details. The mud, brick, slate, pavements and shrubs are all uniformly black. A mass display of soap is seen as inappropriate in a grocer's shop and only the most tart of fruit appear in the greengrocer's window. The 'green and raspberry' colours of the chapel's stained glass are deliberately unappealing, continuing this idea of sharp unripeness, and the tawdry cinema is 'a plaster-and-gilt horror'. The personified Congregational chapel is competitive and snobby, 'thinking itself superior', as if the views of society work into the very materials of its buildings, but all aspirations are stunted: the chapel has a steeple, 'but not a very high one'. The school is damned with faint praise: it is 'all very imposing' and expensive but seen as another contaminated institution condemning children, by implication, to indoctrination and restraint; its architecture mixes 'the suggestion of a chapel and a prison'. All the hopes invested in this society, whether towards enjoyment (the cinema), spiritual yearnings (the chapels), or the education of its children (the school), are condemned as hopelessly vulgar or debased.

Consider how things would be if the sun was out; if the produce in the shops was less tart and more inviting; if the hats and soap were seen as an indication of the greater affluence and cleanliness of working people; if the cinema was seen as a new and exciting medium of expression reaching a new, much wider public; if the aspirations and moral dignity of Nonconformity were dwelt on rather than its most negative aspects; if the new school was seen as the expression of an expansive and dynamic society that cared for its children's education, rather than as a wish to jail and stunt. Then I think the bias and jaundiced partialness of Lawrence's vision becomes apparent. This is a symbolic landscape, a sterile wasteland expressing all of Lawrence's deepest fears about the direction of modern life. Similarly subject to Clifford, Connie's body is also sterile, and it is out of this unvital limbo that she must escape.

Now let us briefly consider Connie in the wood, another of the novel's landscapes:

> She went to the wood next day. It was a grey, still afternoon, with the dark-green dog's-mercury spreading under the hazel copse, and all the trees making a silent effort to open their buds. Today she could almost feel it in her own body, the huge heave of the sap in the massive trees, upwards, up, up to the bud-tips, there to push into little flamey oak-leaves, bronze as blood. It was like a tide running turgid upwards, and spreading on the sky. (p. 127)

This may not appear so obviously biased, but it is not a simple description of a wood either. This is the place for silence, growth, mystery and, above all, bodily awareness. Connie and the wood move through the seasons together, out of winter, through a protracted spring and into midsummer. They are seen as intimately related. I am sure that you can find many passages for yourself to develop this point. Connie's physical reawakening here is in sympathetic accord with the wood's – both are caught up in an irresistible tidal wave, 'the huge heave of the sap'. One natural process, the breaking of trees into bud, is expressed in terms of another, the breaking of the sea on the shore. The effect is to stress the concord, the rhythm of nature in all its aspects. The effort implied by 'push' and the reference to blood seem to suggest that any new growth is difficult. This is reinforced by the startlingly unnatural idea of water 'running turgid upwards' and 'spreading on the sky'. Birth of any kind may be inevitable but it is not painless or without struggle. The analogy to the human situation, the growing involvement of Connie with Mellors, is clear.

The wood expresses Lawrence's sense of the life force in all living things, but it also has a complex, sophisticated literary heritage. If Lawrence writes about Tevershall as a kind of hell inhabited by lost souls, his descriptions of the wood are equally artificial. We should not be fooled by the accuracy and loving observation he gives to the surface details – in this case the 'dark-green dog's mercury' that is spreading under the hazel trees. The wood passages are Lawrence's contribution to a convention or way of writing about the natural world that goes back to classical antiquity – namely, the 'pastoral'. The pastoral convention is a deliberately artificial way of writing about the countryside, stressing the unfallen simplicity and purity of nature and often contrasting it with the sinful world of social man and his institutions. In other words, it can be used to express a writer's sense of what is and what might, or ought, to be. These conventions have proved very adaptable to changing historical situations and Lawrence mobilises them very effectively in his battle against the evils of the modern industrial world. Pastoral love poetry also associates a natural landscape with a perfect, idealised love outside time and society in a kind of golden-age Garden of Eden. Pastoral conventions can also be used to create a privileged space outside the pressures of society where people can recover and discover themselves before returning to the world. In his own way, Lawrence is drawing on all these possibilities when he writes about Connie and Mellors in the wood. The wood has associations too with the fabulous Sherwood Forest, outlawry, Robin Hood and freedom from repressive laws.

Most important of all, beneath the surface detail an ancient myth is acted out that has nothing do with the 'novel of gossip' and is the true source of the book's authority and power. Folklore, myth and legend of all cultures contain stories of imprisoned or enchanted princesses who must be awakened or released into life. As much as Persephone, Connie is subject to a gloomy underworld king; like Sleeping Beauty, she needs to be awakened by a kiss. The theme of rescue and awakening is a crucial one, and Connie draws much of her appeal from these mythical analogues. Mellors, too, as rescuing 'prince', forms part of this mythical pattern deeply embedded in the text. That is why he must be partially exempt from social determinants. He is a construct to fit the pattern, as Clifford is.

At several points in this section, I have pointed out the strain between Lawrence's impositions on the novel as a form or set of conventions, and the reader's expectations. I have asked you to recognise this as a necessary prerequisite of forming your own critical response. We have seen how the book moves beyond the simply plausible in the areas of characterisation, situation and language, and I have tried to give some explanation of why Lawrence should challenge us in this way. I should like to finish by looking at the ending and at the kind of difficulties it gives Lawrence and us.

In the writing of *Lady Chatterley's Lover*, Lawrence embraces some powerful contradictions. He rewrites an old story with a mixture of simple directness and artful complexity. He shapes a modern fable out of ancient mythical material yet gives it the surface details of a naturalistic novel. This attempt to hold together different levels of reality in a precarious synthesis runs into difficulties when the lovers leave the wood. Modern novels, unlike fairy stories, cannot end 'happily ever after' in a manner that might satisfy children or an unsophisticated listener. The modern reader is aware of the enmeshing complexities and compromises that life forces on us, and expects realistic fiction to take account of them too. Once the lovers leave the wood and move back into time they begin to look vulnerable and weak; the novel too seems to lose its confidence and starts to fragment. The Venice and London scenes seem a bit sketchy and rather uncertain, as Lawrence seeks to gather up the threads. Mellors' interview with Sir Malcolm (pp. 294–5), for example, seems particularly implausible, and those scenes featuring Duncan Forbes (pp. 274–82, 297–9) I find truncated and unsatisfactory. Much of the real narrative is now marginalised and takes place 'off stage' in letters; indeed the book ends with a letter as if to stress the personal and vulnerable nature of Lawrence's hopes for the future.

It is important to recognise that such an ending is not the result of impatience or the loss of energy in a dying man but the inevitable consequence of unresolved tensions that have been present in the book throughout. The ending merely exposes them. Lawrence cannot work with society but only against it. This absolute split between the individual and society is present even in the closing paragraphs, where Mellors projects his vision of how society ought to be into some nebulous utopian future; for the present, there is only some measure of personal salvation.

The novel, however, is a social and compromising form of literature and, once the lovers have left the protection of the wood, it forces its social compromises on Lawrence. Connie and Mellors can bring life to themselves but they cannot bring life to a sick and dying civilisation. The mythic pattern that Lawrence has drawn from ancient fertility rites cannot be completed. There is prophecy and vision in Lawrence's last novel, but no social programme that could link his lovers with others in the community to work for a better future. So Lawrence is forced to resort to the limited and evasive comforts of those old-fashioned novels he despises. In order to complete or 'close' his book, the challenge to the social order that he has invested in the rebellious pair has to be muted or marginalised. Connie and Mellors escape from society to find fulfilment on a farm, but they are still sustained by Connie's private income: to this extent they are dependent on a society they hate but are powerless to change.

On a personal level, Lawrence's plea that we keep warmth and vitality alive in our lives is one that we can surely assent to; as a piece of social criticism, *Lady Chatterley's Lover* invites a more ambiguous and divided response. It is the final paradox in a book full of contradictions that this most assertive and dogmatic of fictions should end on such a compromised and melancholy note.

7

How to write an essay on Lawrence

Constructing an essay

OF COURSE, there is no one way to write well on Lawrence or any major author, but he does present some problems for those of us trying to write a satisfactory critical essay. Some of these pitfalls are common to all essays written on novelists, but Lawrence seems to present them in a particularly exaggerated way.

Here is a typical Lawrence question on *Sons and Lovers*

> Would you describe Paul's mother as portrayed by Lawrence in *Sons and Lovers* as 'a blight on his life'? Give reasons for your answer.

Now, this is a question about the novel's content broadly based on an analysis of one of the main characters. It is a common-enough question to ask about a novel, and it is also a question that it is easy to do badly. The temptation is to throw down indiscriminately everything you know about Mrs Morel in rough chronological order, starting with her early married life and ending the essay with her death. In effect you are retelling her story in your own way as if it were real life, forgetting that the novel is a *text*, a structured, crafted piece of writing. This is fatally easy to do with the discussion of any novel, and this is why novels are often written about badly, even though they are sometimes more fun to study than poems and plays. This kind of approach will produce a long, over-general and shapeless essay that will get poor marks even though it is obvious that you have read the novel, enjoyed it and know a lot about Mrs Morel.

Another pitfall is the reverse of this, and sometimes made by clever, ambitious students. You might have become intrigued by the relationship between Mrs Morel and Paul. You've read a lot of criticism of the novel – perhaps too much – and this has given you a great deal of contradictory material and advice about Paul's 'Oedipus complex', his inability to make other satisfactory relationships while his mother lives. The danger here is that you will go into the essay confused in your own mind and write an answer that loses sight of the text altogether. Instead, you will produce a lot of crude psychoanalysis using the relationship of Paul and his mother as a case-history for a theory rather than directing your attention to what actually happens in the novel. Because *Sons and Lovers* is partly autobiographical, another temptation allied to this is to get drawn into a discussion of Lawrence's own life and problems as a reason for writing the book. Again, this biographical material is of secondary importance; you will get marked down for irrelevance and for not answering the question. You must go back to the text and show that you recognise the ambiguity and the complexity of the relationship as it is expressed in Lawrence's own writing. You must write directly on specific incidents and episodes, responding to the text's richness as honestly as you can.

Let us look at the question again. What you must not do is stop reading after 'describe Paul's mother' and simply put down everything you know about Mrs Morel. Read the question carefully, pause, and ask yourself, 'What is the examiner looking for here?' Is this question just about Mrs Morel? No. It is about the relationship between Paul and his mother, so he must get as much attention as she does. If you have thought about the novel at all, it must be evident to you that the quotation is both true and untrue. Undoubtedly, Mrs Morel is a 'blight on Paul's life', but then you have to ask yourself, 'All the time? In every part of the book?' Clearly there is a complexity and an ambiguous tension in the relationship that helps make the novel as good as it is. The examiner is after an answer aware of this fact and drawing upon details of specific episodes to illustrate it. Already in your mind you begin to see the possible shape of your answer: Mrs Morel has many distinctive qualities; she is jealously possessive of her son and finds it difficult to let him go, but she also gives him ambition, respect for the intellect and 'urges him into life'. There is a paradox here that your essay must expose and exploit, so *begin planning your essay with the question.* Every essay must have an introductory paragraph that responds to the question, examines it and even seeks to challenge its assumptions on occasions. The next state is to jot down two or three episodes you know well to illustrate both the negative and positive side of Mrs Morel's love for her son. These will provide the substance of your essay. Try to choose episodes that are evenly phased through the book. Think of each episode as providing a paragraph. You should now have a sense of the likely development of your answer, where you are going to start and finish, though some of the details and amplifications may only come to you as you go along. Now, and only now, you are ready to begin writing.

By giving yourself a little bit of time to think and plan you will be less likely to write the essay you would like to have written as opposed to the one that is actually set. You will also be less tempted to put down all you know rather than what is most pertinent to the question. You will be in control of your material and this will be evident to the examiner. Beginnings and endings of essays are very important, because they can tell any reader just that. A poor essay is one that wastes time for a page or two by retelling the story of Lawrence's life or some such evasion before trying to engage the question. This is a very common failing: most opening paragraphs are redundant. Another weakness is the essay that just stops or lamely concludes in mid-stride by repeating the question. A good concluding paragraph is most unlikely to be a simple yes or no. In a good essay you should be persuading yourself of your case as you go along, so the ending seems increasingly inevitable. Your conclusion should not be over-elaborate, but it should return to the question, usually suggesting some modification, or that the question should be placed in a wider perspective because it is too simple or limiting as it stands. Let me try to summarise these points. A well-constructed essay must have

1 *an opening paragraph that engages with the question;*
2 *subsequent paragraphs that develop an argument in response to the issues raised by the question, supported by detailed, accurate knowledge of the text;*
3 *a concluding paragraph that returns to the question and reconsiders it in the light of your discussion.*

Preparing for an exam essay

If you are studying Lawrence for an exam, the sort of essay you can expect to be asked to write is really quite predictable; for any writer there are, after all, only a small number of substantial topics that are suitable for examination purposes. Of course, you should make sure that you have information on the main characters, but with Lawrence be sure to have something to say on his whole new conception of what constitutes 'character'. Similarly you need material on the relationships in Lawrence's novels, but you also need to explain why he focuses on the emotional and sexual to the exclusion of other aspects of life. As with any novelist, you have things to say about the novel's wider, social community and the way the main characters relate to their society, but nature is particularly significant for Lawrence too; characters invariably relate to each other in and through nature. Be able to illustrate and comment on that. Lawrence's distinctive use of language – his characteristic 'style' – is also clearly important, and you should give special attention to the symbolism that he employs both to explore complex areas of experience and as an organising device for texts as a whole. It is always helpful to have some ideas on the narrative structure and overall 'shape' of the novel you are studying, and to be able to relate important episodes in the text to this wider organisation. Finally, you need some sense of Lawrence's view on life in general – why he has written the novel in the way he has, and what values the book expresses. Exam questions on Lawrence can be phrased in many different ways, but with material on the various major aspects of the novel you will be well prepared. *Think about the issues* and how best to illustrate them. You need to be flexible in an exam; merely memorising class notes and old essays is *not* good preparation.

Types of questions

Essay questions are often built around an antithesis or contrast, either stated or implied. The question on Mrs Morel that we began with invited discussion on her relationship with Paul. The suggestion put forward by the quotation was that the relationship was bad for Paul, but the way the question was phrased implied there might be alternative ways of seeing this relationship. Here is another question on *Sons and Lovers*, and in this case the antithesis is more clear-cut.

> 'Poetic force', 'Social realism': which of these aspects of Lawrence's writing is most powerfully present in *Sons and Lovers*?

This is more difficult than the first question because it is asking not just for knowledge of the content of the novel but also for appreciation of its aesthetic qualities – the manner in which it is written. Still, exactly the same principles apply. Interrogate the question. Ask yourself what exactly is meant by 'poetic force' and how you would illustrate it. The way the question is phrased implies that this aspect of Lawrence's writing is somehow different from his 'social realism'. You need in your opening paragraph to define what you think is meant by these terms so that you can use them to your satisfaction and advantage. The examiner must have no doubts about how you interpret the question. You might argue that Lawrence's 'poetic force' is most evident when he is examining his characters' most intimate psychological conflicts and experiences, usually when they are in close contact with nature and often using symbolism drawn from the natural world. 'Social realism', you might go on, refers more to Lawrence's skill in depicting the exterior world of everyday life and more ordinary experiences. You would need to say something like this and then go on to map out your essay by thinking of two or three likely episodes to illustrate this distinction. You might choose the passage where Mrs Morel is locked out of the house under the brilliant moon with the tall perfumed lilies, or the episode where Paul makes love to Clara in the fields and hears the peewits call. 'Social realism' might be illustrated by examining a scene of family tension or Paul's interview at Jordan's. Having chosen your scenes, you need to discuss them in detail, commenting on their respective strengths and what they bring to the novel as a whole. You then need a concluding paragraph that picks up the notion of 'powerfully present'. You might argue that, because Lawrence's poetic talent is so pronounced and unusual, this is the more dominant aspect of his fiction. Or you might say that he shifts and changes: the first half of the novel is dominated by 'social realism' but the second by 'poetic force'. Or you might argue that the distinction is too arbitrary and clear-cut: the poetry has 'force' because it is rooted in observable reality and the 'social realism' is so powerfully presented because Lawrence has the poet's eye for the vivid, evocative image. It doesn't matter which of these conclusions you reach provided you argue from a detailed knowledge of particular passages. This is the only way to make sharp points and give your discussion direction and purpose.

When examiners want you to discuss the language of a Lawrence novel, they often set an extended question using long quotations. Here is an example:

> Using the following extracts as a starting-point, consider Lawrence's portrayal of Mr Morel and his significance in *Sons and Lovers*:
>
> 1 Therefore, the dusky, golden softness of this man's sensuous flame of life, that flowed off his flesh like the flame from a candle, not baffled and gripped into incandescence by thought and spirit as her life was, seemed to her something wonderful, beyond her.
>
> 2 The collier's small mean head, with its black hair slightly soiled with grey, lay on the bare arms, and the face, dirty and inflamed, with a fleshy nose and thin, paltry brows, was turned sideways, asleep with beer and weariness and nasty temper.

This question is looking for a character analysis of Mr Morel but with particular references to Lawrence's method of presentation. The quotations are there to help you; with essays of this kind it is important to work at the passages and not be in too much of a hurry to move on to a general essay. You could discuss the lyricism of the first piece, how it shows that the young Gertrude Coppard cannot resist the exotic mystery and spontaneous energy of the young miner expressed in the image of the candle flame. You could then go on to examine the appropriateness of this image: live flame is fascinating but also unpredictable and dangerous; candles give off heat and light but exhaust themselves in the process; all this is true of Walter Morel. He is not 'gripped' by thought and spirit as his wife is; he lacks her 'incandescent' will, and so his flame gutters and finally goes out. The second quotation shows Walter's fine energy turned inwards, self-destructively, upon itself. It also provides evidence for the negative bias of much of the description of Walter after his marriage, with the emphasis now on dirt, intoxication and disgruntled animality, all in a tone of sour disapproval. Walter is now critically distanced by the narrator. He is just 'the collier', his head is 'small' and 'mean', and his white hair, rather than evoking pity, is 'slightly soiled' and thus unattractive. You could work through all the details of the quotations in this way. Once you have brought out the ambiguity in Lawrence's presentation of Walter in these passages, you can move on to discuss others that show the positive and negative sides of his nature. Notice that the question does not just ask for a discussion of Mr Morel's character; it asks you to consider *how* Lawrence portrays him and his significance for the book *as a whole*. The more subtle answer would choose scenes that appear to show Walter in a bad light but on closer examination reveal a more sympathetic portrait despite the narrator's bias against him. For example, I am reminded of the funny episode when he offers his sweaty singlet to the startled clergyman visiting Mrs Morel for tea. His wasteful vitality is a constant challenge and threat to the middle-class cultural values and aspirations of Mrs Morel and Paul. You might conclude that he is the most significant expression of a disruptive energy that Lawrence never manages to accommodate or come to terms with in this novel.

Another common type of question is the evaluative statement, often in the form of a short, contentious quotation on which you are asked to comment or discuss. Here are two examples:

> 'The title of *The Rainbow* provides a key to its meaning.' Discuss.
>
> 'A study of disintegration.' Do you agree with this description of *Women in Love*?

This kind of essay question gives you much more freedom to shape your essay, but there are dangers in this. Beware of woolly discussiveness. It is very easy, when attempting to abstract Lawrence's 'philosophy' or discuss his ideas, to do so in vague, general terms that draw you further and further away from the texts themselves. Ask yourself what you can use from the text to give your opinions some substance and organisation. The first of these questions is about the symbolism of *The Rainbow* and how it is linked to its theme. Rainbow symbolism occurs at points of crisis in the lives of all three generations of the Brangwen family, and the most important instance comes in the final paragraphs of the novel. If you have a grasp of where and how the symbolism is used and can discuss it, your essay will fall into shape. Your introduction might discuss the themes of quest, regeneration, discovery and renewal in *The Rainbow*. You could suggest that these themes are expressed by a whole set of symbols involving arches and doorways, and that the rainbow, though only one of these, is clearly the most important. The main body of your essay would discuss examples and your conclusion might broadly agree with the question and try to explain why the rainbow is such a significant symbol for Lawrence.

The problem with the second essay is that it is easy just to agree with the quotation, and this does not make for a very critical essay. Maybe the thing to do would be to make some distinction between Lawrence's overall view of the sickness of modern life, particularly as it is expressed in Gerald's breakdown, and the hope he tries to find through Birkin's relationship with Gerald and Ursula. Again, your argument needs to be rooted in particular passages and episodes. You might conclude that *Women in Love* is indeed 'a study of disintegration', but that disintegration is often necessary before fresh growth can take place.

How to use quotations

Quotations have varying uses but they are no substitute for your own work. Nothing will annoy an examiner quicker than indiscriminate quotation that shows nothing or goes nowhere. One use of quotations is to support your points by giving collaborating evidence; they show your command of textual detail and should be as short as possible. Often just a phrase will be sufficient, and you can draw such references into your developing argument as you go along. Be selective; use the best quotation to illustrate your point, not all you might have used. Judicious selection can give an examiner a very good sense of a candidate's ability: indiscriminate quotation soon brings rapidly diminishing returns and is a waste of time and energy.

Sometimes quotations provide a quick and easy into a problem or can serve to clinch an argument. For example, you might want to discuss Walter Morel. A quotation such as 'He had denied the God in him', which is short and easily memorable, opens up several lines of discussion. You could use it to explore authorial bias, asking what Lawrence means by 'God' in this instance and whether, or in what sense, the statement is true. Similarly, a pithy, short quotation can provide a neat summary, a tidy and precise way of rounding off your argument.

There is a place for the extended quotation, especially when you are involved in any discussion of style or Lawrence's use of symbolism. If you were examining a character's development, a longer quotation could be very useful for, say, a careful, close examination of some psychological moment of crisis. But a quotation of any length *must* be discussed, not just left to speak for itself. The reader must not be left in any doubt why you have chosen it. Also you must quote accurately; sloppy misquotation can undermine your argument and gives a bad impression. Accuracy in quotation, as in spelling, punctuation and other matters of formal presentation, all help to establish the confidence of the examiner in your work overall.

Writing commentaries: a final note

Some examination boards favour the use of the extended passage for commentary as a means of testing their candidates' abilities to respond to the language of a writer. Again, don't panic but read the passage carefully and ask yourself why this particular extract has been chosen. Commentary questions often direct you towards certain attributes or qualities in the passage that the examiner wishes you to discuss. Remember, any work you do, however excellent, that doesn't engage directly with the passage in front of you is a complete waste of time and won't get you any marks. It is much better to write something that is careful, detailed and structured, showing that you have worked through the passage in a methodical manner before you begin, than launch out on a wild, sporadic paraphrase with critical impressions and afterthoughts thrown in that makes it clear that you have not really thought out your answer at all. You may get some marks this way, but you will never get good marks and you will miss a great deal. Commentaries should be easier to do than exam essays, but invariably they are done much worse, because candidates dislike having to confront a text and respond directly to it without the aid of previously prepared material. Nevertheless, this is what you must learn to do. This book has been based on the critical analysis of selected passages. If you follow the procedures I have laid down, or others like them, you will be surprised – and pleased – to see how much you can discover and express for yourself. The purpose of this book has been to try to give you confidence and set you free to discover your own responses to a challenging and stimulating writer. Studying and writing about Lawrence is hard work, but it can be rewarding and very enjoyable too.

Further reading

Books by Lawrence

THE BULK of Lawrence's writing is readily available in Penguin books. The major novels, in Penguin Classics, all have excellent introductions, suggestions for further reading and useful notes. If you are studying Lawrence, these are the best texts to buy. One very enjoyable way of getting a better understanding of Lawrence is to read more Lawrence, not just more of his fiction but his essays, letters and autobiographical sketches too. His thoughts about the novel are particularly interesting: 'Morality and the Novel', 'Why the Novel Matters' and 'Surgery for the Novel – or a Bomb' can most easily be found in *A Selection from 'Phoenix'* (1971), edited by A. A. H. Inglis, or in *Selected Literary Criticism* (1956), edited by Anthony Beal. 'A Propos of *Lady Chatterley's Lover*', a useful supplement to the novel, can also be found in the Inglis volume.

Books about Lawrence

If you are interested in Lawrence's life, the standard biography is *Priest of Love: Life of D. H. Lawrence* (1974) by Harry T. Moore, also cheaply available in Penguin. A book to dip into is the three-volume composite biography by Edward Nehls (1957–9). This contains many brief reminiscences of Lawrence by those who knew him and is full of useful information.

Critical books on Lawrence's fiction

You can get a sense of the early reception of Lawrence's work from *D. H. Lawrence: The Critical Heritage* (1970), edited by R. P. Draper. A major reassessment of his achievement began in the 1950s with the publication of *D. H. Lawrence, Novelist* (1955) by F. R. Leavis, and Graham Hough's *The Dark Sun: A Study of D. H. Lawrence* (1956).

These are still influential books, the former an important work by a major literary critic. Keith Sagar's book *The Art of D. H. Lawrence* (1966) is influenced by Leavis and based on close attention to passages and Lawrence's 'poetic method'. H. M. Daleski's *The Forked Flame* (1965) pays more attention to Lawrence's philosophy and ideas, while Julian Moynahan's *The Deed of Life: The Novels and Tales of D. H. Lawrence* (1966) is particularly good for Lawrence's new theory of character and his evolving sense of literary form. Frank Kermode's little book *Lawrence* (1973) in Fontana's 'Modern Masters' series is a marvel of compressed scholarship and shrewd judgement. *D. H. Lawrence: The World of the Major Novels* by Scott Sanders, also published in 1973, is valuable for its historical, social analysis. If you are interested in a feminist critique of Lawrence, Kate Millet's *Sexual Politics* (1971) is where you start; it is a very challenging and stimulating pioneer work. 1979 produced two contrasting books: John Worthen's wide-ranging *D. H. Lawrence and the Idea of the Novel* examines Lawrence's relationship with his contemporary readers and his changing notions of what a novel should be; Charles L. Ross's *The Composition of 'The Rainbow' and 'Women in Love'* provides a detailed analysis of the textual evolution of Lawrence's two major novels. Finally, two more difficult books for the advanced student: Colin Clarke's *River of Dissolution: D. H. Lawrence and English Romanticism* (1969), which examines Lawrence's inheritance from the Romantic poets; and *D. H. Lawrence: History, Ideology and Fiction* (1982) by Graham Holderness. This is a sophisticated, Marxist examination of Lawrence's artistic development in the context of labour history and the effect of the First World War. Both provide an interesting challenge to Leavis's reading of the fiction. Graham Holderness has also produced an excellent book on *Women in Love* in the Open University Press's 'Open Guides to Literature' series (1986).

Collections on individual novels

There are Macmillan casebooks on *Sons and Lovers* (1969), edited by Gāmini Salgādo, and *'The Rainbow' and 'Women in Love'* (1969), edited by Colin Clarke. Both have valuable essays as well as extracts from the books already mentioned. In particular, the Salgādo collection has two seminal essays on *Sons and Lovers* – Mark Schorer's 'Technique as Discovery' (*Hudson Review*, 1948), and Dorothy Van Ghent's 'On *Sons and Lovers*', reprinted from her book *The English Novel: Form and Function* (1953).

How to use criticism

Criticism can be a good servant but is a bad master. Don't move into secondary material on a novel until you have thought about it and worked out some ideas for yourself. All criticism is partial, subject to the writer's prejudice and the constraints of the time when it was written. It is also part of a developing debate that is never-ending. Learn to criticise the critic; try to sort out his or her line and position. Don't read too much criticism – it will only confuse you – but don't read just one critic either; it is likely to bias you unduly. This is particularly true when a novel is new to you. It is best if you can find opposing opinions and then test them against your own response and mediate between them if necessary. It is exhilarating to find a critic supporting your own hunches and good when the strength of someone else's arguments forces you back to the texts, but, remember, in the end it is your own reading that is the most interesting, and the one that matters.